History
History
TODAY

Kateryn Parr
The Nursing Mother
of the Reformation

Hannah Stone

DayOne

ISBN 978-1-84625-766-7

British Library Cataloguing in Publication Data available

Published by Day One Publications
Ryelands Road, Leominster, HR6 8NZ
Telephone 01568 613 740 FAX 01568 611 473
email—sales@dayone.co.uk
website—www.dayone.co.uk

Cover design by Kathryn Chedgzoy
Printed by 4edge

For John and Kathryn Roberts, without
whom this book may not have existed!

Endorsements

A number of years ago while preaching near Westbury, Wiltshire, I met a young lady called Hannah Stone. Her father wrote a book about Hannah entitled, Too Young To Die. *Hanna has now written a book about another young lady who, from a human point was also 'too young to die'. Her name was Kateryn Parr, wife of Henry VIII.*

I was delighted to meet Hannah because we both had an interest in the Tudors. There was, however, one wife of Henry, Kateryn Parr, that I longed to know more about, so I encouraged Hannah to supply me with the information. I was so pleased that her hard and diligent work is to be published by Day One.

Katheryn Parr was a Christian lady who played a major role in bringing Christianity to the nation. I am delighted Hannah has taken the time to provide us with a biography that was worthy of writing, for it causes us to be thankful that, as in Caesar's household, so in the household of Henry VIII, Almighty God is never left without witness and the Christian influence is clearly evident.

This book is warm, very well written and brings the whole period to life. It feels as though you are living among them. It takes you on a journey with Kateryn Parr and you are disappointed when the journey ends. It is a book you do not want to put down.

John G. Roberts

This wonderful little book gives some fascinating insights into the life of an important Christian in Tudor history. It is well known how Elizabeth I played an important role in the Reformation, but what Hannah helpfully explains is that, through God's providence, Kateryn had an important influence on the faith of Elizabeth when she was a child.

Prof. Stuart Burgess

Acknowledgements

My thanks to John Roberts for first putting the idea into my head to write this book, to Helen Clark for her hard work on the editing and my parents for their support.

Contents

Contents

Timeline

Day	Month	Year	Event
28	June	1491	Henry VIII born.
12	April	1509	Henry VIII crowned.
11	June	1509	Henry VIII marries Catherine of Aragon.
		1512	Kateryn Parr born.
		1513	Brother, William Parr, born.
		1515	Sister, Anne Parr, born.
18	February	1516	Mary (later Mary I) born.
	Autum	1517	Father, Thomas Parr, dies.
	Spring	1529	Kateryn marries Edward Borough.
		1531	Mother, Maud Parr, dies.
14	November	1532	Henry VIII marries Anne Boleyn in a secret ceremony.
23	May	1533	Henry's marriage to Catherine of Aragon annulled.
	Spring	1533	Edward Borough dies.
7	September	1533	Elizabeth (later Elizabeth I) is born and Mary is declared illegitimate.
		1534	Kateryn marries Lord John Latimer.
		1534	Act of Supremacy announces Henry VIII as 'Supreme Head of the Church of England'
17	May	1536	Elizabeth declared illegitimate.
19	May	1536	Anne Boleyn is executed.
30	May	1536	Henry VIII marries Jane Seymour.
1	October	1536	Uprising in Louth, Lincolnshire, which leads to the Pilgrimage of Grace.
11	October	1536	Latimer takes the oath of the Pilgrimage of Grace.
	January	1537	Kateryn and two stepchildren taken hostage at Snape Castle.
12	October	1537	Edward (later Edward VI) is born.

24	October	1537	Jane Seymour dies.
6	January	1540	Henry VIII marries Anne of Cleves.
9	July	1540	Henry's marriage to Anne of Cleves is annulled.
28	July	1540	Henry VIII marries Catherine Howard.
14	February	1542	Catherine Howard is executed.
	February	1543	Lord Latimer dies.
12	July	1543	Kateryn marries Henry VIII.
	February	1544	'Act of Succession' includes both Mary and Elizabeth in the line of succession.
	April	1544	*Psalms or Prayers* published.
11	July	1544	Kateryn proclaimed Regent of England.
14	September	1544	Boulogne surrenders to Henry VIII.
	October	1544	Henry VIII returns from France.
	June	1545	Anne Askew arrested as part of an attempt to bring down Kateryn.
	June	1545	*Prayers or Meditations* published.
		1546	Anne Askew imprisoned in Newgate.
26	July	1546	Anne Askew burnt at the stake.
	Summer	1546	Near arrest of Kateryn.
28	January	1547	Henry VIII dies and Edward VI becomes king.
	May?	1547	Kateryn marries Thomas Seymour.
5	November	1547	*Lamentation of a Sinner* published.
31	January	1548	Translation of *Erasmus' Paraphrases on the New Testament* published.
30	August	1548	Daughter, Mary Seymour, born.
5	September	1548	Kateryn dies of puerperal fever.
7	September	1548	Kateryn's funeral service led by Miles Coverdale.

Preface

I t all started with a Sunday lunchtime chat. John Roberts, the retired managing director of Day One Publications, and his wife, Kathryn, were at our house—John having been booked as our church's preacher for the day. One of the many subjects that came up for discussion was the fact that Anne Boleyn, Henry VIII's second wife, was a Christian. Then it was mentioned that Kateryn Parr, his sixth wife, was also a Christian. Whether I had been aware of this before the meal I'm not sure, but God had planted a seed that led to further interest in Kateryn. Sometimes Kateryn can be portrayed as nothing more than a survivor, with some going a bit further, portraying her as a nurse to Henry as well. But, having read Faith Cook's two books on Lady Jane Grey (*Lady Jane Grey: Nine Day Queen of England*[1](a biography) and *Caught in the Web*[2] (historical fiction)), in which Kateryn plays a major role, I became increasingly aware that this woman was far more than just another of Henry's six wives. Kateryn deserved far more interest than we sometimes give her. However, at the time I went no further with any research.

A few years later, I went to university to do a history degree, and the time came to think about a dissertation topic. I knew I wanted to do something regarding the Reformation, as I have always loved that period of history where we see God spread his light across Europe, but what? Then, I had the thought of writing something to do with Kateryn Parr, Lady Jane Grey and the Reformation. (Unfortunately, due to space limitations Lady Jane was dropped at the very first meeting with my supervisor!) However, I soon had a title: 'How Far did Kateryn Parr influence the English Reformation?' This was a great title as far as the lecturers were concerned—it had a fresh angle on the subject of the English Reformation and, being about a woman, gave it more *kudos*. Over the course of my third year at university, I read more of Kateryn and explored her life and achievements. I came to understand more and more about how *God* used this amazing woman for his purposes in the Tudor court. Perhaps, far from just being a survivor, God used Kateryn to shape the future direction of a whole country. I have come to admire her so much that I cannot wait to meet her in heaven. (That is one of the great things about studying history as a Christian; rather than being long-dead people who we have to study, some historical figures transform into our Christian brothers and sisters whom we will one day meet!) However, a university dissertation cannot give any credit to God and so it had to be all about what Kateryn and others did, with no acknowledgement of the Sovereign Lord. But now, I want to clearly show how God used a woman to fulfil his purposes, even though her actions were mostly behind the scenes.

I wrote this book in the hope of encouraging you; God has his behind-the-scenes workers. Kateryn never achieved the publicity of Calvin, Luther, Tyndale or any of the other 'frontline' workers, but God still used her, sometimes in a very quiet way, for his aims. We are all part of God's story and each of us play an important part in its unfolding. I want to encourage you that, though you may never know the full impact of your life living for God, it does not mean there is none. Kateryn had an incredible impact, particularly on Henry's two children, Edward and Elizabeth, but never lived to see the entire reign of Edward or see Elizabeth even succeeding to the throne, never mind the 'golden age' of Elizabeth. Yet, as we shall see, her influence meant that the two reigns were those where God's Word was spread throughout England. Who knows what impact we may have on others around us and how God may use that to further his Kingdom? I pray this book will be an encouragement and spur all of us, both men and women, to live for God and be willing to be used for him wherever he sends us.

Because of the distance in time between us and Kateryn, we cannot know everything for certain. In fact, even where and when she was born is debatable. What I present here is what I have come to think, based on my reading both in that year of university study and since. At the end of this book there is a bibliography which lists various books you may wish to read to get a more comprehensive understanding of her life and times.

As with all aspects of history, there is always debate and argument, especially when dealing with events in the distant past, and the few sources we have may be affected by bias. What I have attempted to do is present the facts of those events that played a part in Kateryn's life, for example the Pilgrimage of Grace in 1536. It should not be taken as a historical analysis, as there is no room for that here.

Notes

1 Cook, Faith, *Lady Jane Grey: Nine Day Queen of England*, (Welwyn Garden City: Evangelical Press, 2004).
2 Cook, Faith, *Caught in the Web: A Tale of Tudor Times*, (Welwyn Garden City: Evangelical Press, 2006).

Introduction

In February 1543, a court observer noted that Henry VIII was visiting his daughter Mary and her ladies in waiting two or three times a day.[1] But why should he visit his daughter in a way that he had not done so before? Perhaps the answer lay with Lady Latimer? Kateryn Latimer née Parr had recently come to court and had become an attendant to Mary. Henry ordered fashionable mourning attire for her and her stepdaughter when her husband died in March, and soon it became obvious why he was so attentive. On the 12th of July, Henry (fifty-two) and Kateryn (thirty-one) were married at Hampton Court—Kateryn becoming his sixth wife. What might Kateryn have been thinking as Stephen Gardiner, Bishop of Westminster and Winchester, read out the service? After all, the man she was promising to obey and serve had now heard the marriage service a total of six times. Two of his wives had been divorced: one because she could not produce an heir, and one, apparently, because she was not beautiful enough. Two others had been executed on charges of adultery. And here she stood, binding herself to this man in marriage.

But this was not Kateryn's first marriage either and, unlike Henry's previous wife (Catherine Howard who was only nineteen when she married Henry), Kateryn had plenty of 'life experience'. In fact, Henry was her third husband and, after he died, Kateryn would marry again, becoming the most married queen consort in English history. She had lived in the distant North with her first husband and had been held as a hostage in the Pilgrimage of Grace in 1536, when married to her second. Her first two husbands were not from the top echelons of the aristocracy, and she had never been part of the limelight of court till now. But, with her marriage to Henry, Kateryn became the highest lady in the land.

Historians may attribute Henry's marriage to Kateryn to him looking for a mature wife, who could look after him and she just happened to be a lady-in-waiting to his daughter, the future Mary I. But, as queen, Kateryn would go on to have such an influence on the progress of the English Reformation that Agnes Strickland, a nineteenth-century historical writer, would refer to her as 'the nursing mother of the Reformation'—hence the title of this book.[2] Surely it was *God* who brought her to this exalted position. In fact, it could be said that Kateryn's story would go on to mirror that of Esther's in the Bible. After all, there are some similarities. A woman attracts the eye of a king, a king who has managed to dispose of his previous wife and who is known for his varying tempers. Then, through her exalted position as queen, she saves God's people. Now Kateryn would not save masses of Protestants from being burnt at the stake, but her influence on two of Henry's children, Edward and Elizabeth, would cement their Protestant faith and contribute to the shape of England during their reigns in which the Reformation would continue to spread. To paraphrase Mordecai's words from Esther chapter 5, she had come to a royal position for such a time as this.

But, when Kateryn was born, there was no indication that this woman would grow up to be a servant of God, and certainly not that she would become *queen* of England.

Notes

1 Mueller, Janel [Ed.], *Katherine Parr: Complete Works and Correspondence*, (London: University of Chicago Press, 2011), p. 10.
2 Strickland, Agnes, *Lives of the Queens of England, Volume 5*, (London: Bloomsbury Academic, 1845), p. 2.

1 Her birth and childhood

Kateryn came from a northern, knightly family—a family of good lineage and well established at court. The family's wealth came from sheep. Back in the fourteenth century, the Parr family were members of the household of John of Gaunt, Edward III's third son. During the chaos of the Wars of the Roses in the fifteenth century, they gave their loyalty to the Yorkist side. Despite losing one member of the family on the battlefield, they gambled on Edward of York (who became Edward IV) and won. Rewards followed, and Sir William Parr, the patriarch of the family, was appointed the 'comptroller' of the royal household—the man who controlled all of the king's private expenditure. Over the years the family had managed to keep strong links to the royal court. Lady Elizabeth Parr, Kateryn's grandmother, acted as lady-in-waiting to Queen Anne, the wife of Richard III.

Kateryn's parents were Sir Thomas and Lady Maud Parr. Thomas was very popular with Henry VIII and was created a Knight of the Bath at his coronation, as well as having his debt of £9000 (around £4.5 million today!) cancelled. He was a considerable landowner in the northeast and northwest of England. Maud Parr was the daughter of a wealthy landowner from Northamptonshire, Sir Thomas Green, who, on his death, left everything to his two daughters, so Maud brought much wealth to Thomas when she married him. She became a lady-in-waiting to Catherine of Aragon and it is possible that Kateryn may have been named after her. (The difference in spelling is because there were very few rules, if any, about spelling in Tudor times. Indeed, there were a number of variants of Kateryn's name used in Tudor times. In this book I've decided to use the spelling she herself used.)

Due to the passing of time, we cannot be entirely sure where Kateryn was born, or indeed in what year. Most likely she was born in 1512, either at Great Kimble, Buckinghamshire or Blackfriars, London. A year later, a son was born to Thomas and Maud, called William, and in 1515, another daughter, Anne, was born. William would go on to join the household of the Duke of Richmond, Henry VIII's illegitimate son and, although he had lands in the North, he would rarely visit them. Anne went to court and served all Henry's queens from the mid-1530s. She later married William Herbert and became the Countess of Pembroke.

Sadly, in 1517, Sir Thomas Parr died at the age of forty. Maud was now a single mother, looking after three children aged five, four and two, and she was only twenty-five herself. It might have been expected that Maud would now marry again, but she did no such thing; instead, she remained a widow for the rest of her life. Perhaps part of the reason for this lies in the property laws surrounding marriage at the time. When a woman married, everything she had became her husband's and, should a woman make a wrong choice, she had a great deal to lose as control of her possessions would become her husband's, making it hard for her to leave him. However, as a widow, Maud had more control over her finances. Other well-born women at the time also stayed as widows for the same reasons.

Maud was a very strong character, and has been described by historians as 'resourceful, determined, intelligent', 'independent, capable and unusually articulate', who acted as 'unchallenged queen' with her children![1] These characteristics of female independence would be passed onto Kateryn, who would, at one point in Henry's reign, act as regent in his absence. As we shall see later, Kateryn would then pass on these virtues to her stepdaughter, Elizabeth. Here is perhaps a good example of God working out his plan in advance: as a young child Kateryn was being shown the virtues she would need for her God-given task.

For Maud, the education of her children was extremely important and so she set up a school in her house to educate both hers and other peoples' children. This was also a pragmatic choice: by involving more pupils, she could afford better quality tuition for them and cultivate the ties of kinship that were very important in the Tudor age. As well as Kateryn, Anne and William, the classroom also included their cousins—the four daughters of Kateryn's uncle, Sir William Parr. The approach Maud used was based on the one used by none other than Sir Thomas More, the Lord Chancellor of England from 1529 to 1532. More believed that it was equally valuable to teach girls as it was boys, as 'both have the same human nature and the power of reasoning'.[2] It was more usual for girls to be taught informally in the home by their mothers, receiving religious education and skills to help them be wives and mothers, but not much else. However, as the Tudor age progressed, it started to become more common for girls to be taught to read and write, as many wanted to emulate More, who had three very accomplished daughters. Kateryn would have been taught French—a key skill for court circles—and probably Italian. Scholars differ as to Kateryn's ability in Latin, as no Latin letter written by her survives and, in one letter to her, Prince Edward wrote that he '[heard she] progresses in Latin language'.[3] However, as Edward was able to correspond with Kateryn in Latin, it is clear she had some skill with the language, perhaps learning some as a child and then developing her skill as an adult. Throughout her life, Kateryn had a deep love of learning and a desire for self-improvement. As well as the essential study of the Scriptures, she studied various classical writers, such as Plutarch, Homer and Aristotle. Outside of the classroom, she enjoyed riding, hunting and loved music and dancing, as well as collecting coins and playing chess.

As well as her mother, Kateryn had two other key figures in her life at this time. The first was her uncle, Sir William Parr of Horton. After Sir Thomas' death, William assisted Maud by looking after her lands in the north of England. While he did not have many of the skills to progress at court, it would appear that he was a family man who was held in great affection by his relatives. In a *Book of Hours*[4] that belonged to Thomas and then was given to William, we find inscriptions from Maud, Kateryn and young William, asking Sir William to remember them. Kateryn even wrote a little rhyme: 'Uncle, when you do on this look, I pray you remember who wrote this in your book. Your loving niece Katherine Parr.'[5] There would be a strong bond between uncle and niece for the rest of his life, with William being given an important position in Kateryn's household when she became queen.

The other key player in Kateryn's life at this time was Cuthbert Tunstall, the Bishop of London and later Durham, who shared a grandmother with Kateryn's father, and so was a distant relation. He had a great interest in children and in seeing their development.

Kateryn's education owed a lot to Tunstall's ideas and Maud acknowledged that she valued his advice, to the extent of making him an executor of her will. Perhaps here we see one of God's little ironies with Tunstall and Kateryn having a close connection, as their opinions would soon diverge on the question of a vernacular Bible! As we will see later, Kateryn would go on to be very supportive of having the Bible available in English, even patronizing a project to translate paraphrases of the Bible into English. Tunstall, on the other hand, when Bishop of London, would turn away William Tyndale who wished to translate the Bible into English. He would become more opposed to the Bible being in the vernacular language due to the apparent 'taint' of the connection of a vernacular Bible with that German 'heretic' Luther.[6]

When Kateryn was twelve, Maud started to become concerned, not only with Kateryn's schooling, but also with her marriage. This may appear very young to our modern minds, but with shorter lifespans in Tudor times, things were very different. The time of 'the lover', referred to as the third age by Shakespeare, began around fourteen and generally was considered to last about fourteen years, to the age of twenty-eight. Maud beginning this quest for a husband when Kateryn was just twelve, was due to the fact that finding a husband and negotiating the marriage settlement could take a long time. However, Kateryn's marriage prospects were not great. In his will, her father, Sir Thomas, had left only £400 each to his two girls as a marriage portion—not a very generous amount—and is probably an indication that he expected his two girls to marry respectably, but not impressively. The idea that Kateryn would one day become the highest lady in the land would probably not even have crossed

Maud's mind at this point. In Tudor times, marriage could often be described as a bargain and Maud set out to make the best one she could. The first candidate was Henry Scrope, the grandson of Lord Dacre, to whom Maud appealed to try and arrange the marriage. However, Lord Dacre's son-in-law, Lord Scrope, Henry's father, was against the match as Kateryn was not rich enough. His son's marriage was the only thing that would realistically bring him money and so, he demanded a high price. Lord Dacre tried to persuade Lord Scrope of the benefits of the match. A letter written on the 17th of December 1524 from him to Lord Scrope tried to argue the point, stating that marrying Henry to 'an heir of land' would be 'right costly' and in marrying Kateryn to his son Henry he could avoid this cost, and Henry would benefit from Kateryn's good education.[7] However, Lord Scrope would not be moved and the negotiations fell through. Henry Scrope would then die the following year and, had Kateryn married him, she would have been a widow by the tender age of thirteen.

However, Maud's attentions now turned from Kateryn to her son William, as he was the heir and the one who would continue the Parr name. Maud borrowed money to get a 'good' bride for William—Anne Bourchier (pronounced Bowser). It was hoped that this would bring William her father's title of the Earl of Essex when he died, as well as his wealth, Anne being his only child. However, the marriage was one of the unhappiest on record in the sixteenth century. In 1541, Anne eloped with a lover and child. In 1542, William was legally separated from her and a bill of Parliament meant that Anne's children could not inherit either the Parr or Bourchier lands. The borrowing that Maud had done to bring this ill-fated marriage about, meant there was nothing left to offer with Kateryn's hand. However, at the age of seventeen, probably in the spring of 1529, Kateryn became the bride of Edward Borough, the eldest son of Sir Thomas Borough. For most of the next ten years of her life, Kateryn would be in the North, far away from the court and the South where she had lived.

Notes

1 Mueller, Janel, *Katherine Parr: Complete Works and Correspondence*, p. 5; James, Susan, 'Katherine [Katheryn, Catherine] [née Katherine Parr] (1512–1548)', *Oxford Dictionary of National Biography*, (Oxford University Press, 2004), p.21.

2 Thomas More, quoted in: Porter, Linda, *Katherine the Queen*, (London: Macmillan, 2010), p. 33.

3 Mueller, Janel, *Katherine Parr: Complete Works and Correspondence*, p. 118.

4 *A Book of Hours* was a medieval prayer book which contained set prayers to be read at certain times of the day.

5 Mueller, Janel, *Katherine Parr: Complete Works and Correspondence*, p. 38.

6 Daniell, David, *William Tyndale: A Biography*, (New Haven and London: Yale University Press, 1994), p. 86. For more information on William Tyndale, read: Edwards, Brian H., *God's Outlaw*, (Welwyn Garden City: Evangelical Press, 1981).

7 Whithrow, Brandon, *Katherine Parr: A Guided Tour of the Life and Thought of a Reformation Queen*, (Phillipsburg: P & R Publishing, 2009), p. 134.

2 Marriage to Edward Borough

As the bride of Edward Borough, Kateryn now moved to Gainsborough in Lincolnshire. This would have been a huge move and a very significant change for her. Even for us, a move so many miles from home may be hard and stressful, but for Kateryn this would have been even harder. Lincolnshire was the furthest part of England to be ruled directly from London (the rest of the North being ruled by a Council of the North) and over 150 miles from her London home. Today it may take a few hours for us to drive there and, should our friends or family live there, we can stay in touch via telephone or a social network platform. But, in Tudor times, the distance seemed far greater, taking days to travel. Also, southerners viewed the North through the eyes of ignorance, seeing northerners as unsophisticated in contrast to the pomp and magnificence of court. Henry VIII was recorded as saying that those who occupied the fenlands were less than human![1] It did not help that there was only one main road for travel from the South: the Great North Road. Although the beliefs about the North, that Kateryn would have imbued from others around her, may have been wrong, she still had a lot of adapting to do. She was now many miles away from her family, and most likely she may have found it difficult to adjust.

Kateryn now lived with her husband and her in-laws. Her father-in-law ruled the house and expected obedience from his children. However, his mind was more open when it came to religious matters, and it was perhaps in his house that she first encountered reformed teaching. Kateryn's father-in-law, Sir Thomas Borough, had a reformed chaplain in his house. One historian, Susan James, has suggested that it was here Kateryn came to faith.[2] It is not possible to tell exactly when Kateryn became a Christian, as no document has been left by her with an exact date; however, as many people today do not know when they became a Christian, that may also have been Kateryn's experience. I think it more likely that she became one of God's children when she was Henry's wife, as will be shown when we look into her writings. But God was certainly working in her life, and perhaps preparing the ground for later development during her years as queen.

Two years after their marriage, Kateryn and her husband Edward moved to their own home in Kirton-in-Lindsey, twelve miles from Gainsborough. It is possible that the move was because Kateryn was pregnant, but there is no historical record to back up this supposition. No child would ever result from this union.

In 1531, tragedy struck. Her mother, Maud, died in London at the age of 39. As the woman who brought them up without the aid of their father, she must have been missed greatly by her children. In her will, Maud left Kateryn 'a cross of diamonds with a pendant pearl [and] a cache of loose pearls.'[3] But her other gift to her daughter is perhaps far more interesting, given what Kateryn would go on to become: a jewelled portrait of none other than Kateryn's future husband Henry VIII (as well as that of Catherine of Aragon)! As someone who had been close to Catherine, Maud perhaps wanted Catherine's namesake to have the portraits, particularly as it was becoming more and more apparent that the King's marriage was breaking up. But she could never have imagined when bequeathing her daughter these pictures, that Kateryn would one day become Henry's wife herself, the third one to be called a variant of the name, Kateryn.

Now Kateryn no longer had her mother's guiding hand. And then, just two years later, Edward, Kateryn's husband also died. Now she was a widow at the age of twenty-one. With no child resulting from the union, she had little claim on her in-laws. Her father-in-law gave her a small income but he was much more taken up with his new affairs at court. He had been appointed as chamberlain to Anne Boleyn (Henry's second wife), overseeing her household and he played a big role in the preparations for her coronation. So, as a widow, with little money and no parents to help her, Kateryn disappears from the historical record for twelve months. It is possible that she stayed with family or friends at this time. Cuthbert Tunstall, the father figure of her youth, had been appointed the Bishop of Durham and President of the Council of the North in 1530. There was also the Dowager Lady Strickland, a cousin of Kateryn on her father's side who lived at Sizergh Castle in Cumbria. But wherever she was, God was watching over her and continued to have his hand on her life. When Kateryn was twenty-two, she reappears in the historical record, having married Lord Latimer—a man much older than herself—and so moved to the Yorkshire Dales.

Notes

1 Porter, Linda, *Katherine the Queen*, (London: Macmillan, 2010), p. 50.
2 James, Susan, *Katheryn Parr: The Making of a Queen*, (Aldershot: Ashgate Pub. Ltd, 1999), p. 62.
3 Mueller, Janel, *Katherine Parr: Complete Works and Correspondence*, p. 7.

3 Marriage to Lord Latimer

L ord Latimer was the Member of Parliament for Yorkshire and involved with the Council of the North. This was the administrative centre for the North, with the exception of Lincolnshire. As Latimer had a title, a castle and a role in politics, Kateryn, by marrying him, would be advancing up the social ladder further than her mother might perhaps have expected. He was not an ambitious man. Although he travelled to London to play his part in the ending of parliamentary sessions, he preferred the quiet life—living at home, and managing his estates, which at this time, were in financial difficulties. Lord Latimer had been married twice before, with his previous wife, Elizabeth Musgrave, dying in 1530 after just two years of marriage. He was a man who tried to avoid confrontation, preferring to compromise instead—qualities not lauded in Tudor times, and these would serve him badly in a few years' time. We do not know how the marriage came about, but it was possible that Tunstall and her uncle, Sir William Parr—her father figures—were the key players.

Lord Latimer was more experienced and considerably older than Kateryn when he married her in 1534. He was in his forties, whereas Kateryn was only twenty-two. However, despite this, Kateryn had genuine affection for her husband. They lived together at Snape Castle in North Yorkshire. (If you go to the nearby Thorp Perrow Arboretum, there is a 'Catherine Parr Oak', which is said to have been planted to celebrate their marriage.) In marrying Latimer, Kateryn took on more responsibilities; she now managed a much larger household than that of her first husband and had two children to care for. Latimer had two children from his first marriage: John, who was fourteen, and Margaret, who was nine. So, Kateryn became not just a wife (a role she had played before), but also a stepmother, despite being only twenty-two, and having had, only recently, lost her own mother. But here, once again, we see God's hand at work. Here she was, 'only' stepmother to the future Lord Latimer and a potential wife for one of the nobility of England. In less than ten years, she would be stepmother to the next three rulers of England, and her experience would prove invaluable.

Kateryn and Margaret developed a close relationship with each other. For Margaret, it was her first experience of a loving mother. Kateryn supervised Margaret's studies, encouraged a love of learning, and, perhaps, developed in her a devotion to religion. In her will, Margaret played tribute to how much Kateryn meant to her and how highly she esteemed Kateryn: 'I am never able to render to her grace sufficient thanks for the godly education and tender love and bountiful goodness which I have ever more found in her highness.'[1] (This was written when Kateryn was queen, hence the referring to Kateryn as 'her highness'.) Margaret would later move with Kateryn to court and, when Kateryn married Henry, Margaret was given a place in her household. They never parted until, sadly, Margaret died at the age of twenty-one. In particular, this relationship stood Kateryn in good stead for her relationship with Elizabeth, on whom she would exert a considerable influence.

Sadly, the relationship between Kateryn and her stepson, John, was not nearly so easy and calm. At fourteen, he would perhaps have exhibited signs of what we consider adolescence today, although the idea of being a 'teenager' did not exist in Tudor times. Possibly in later years, when writing her work, *The Lamentation of a Sinner*, she recalled her time with John: 'Younglings and unperfect are offended at small trifles, taking everything in evil part.'[2] With only eight years separating Kateryn and John, and with Kateryn having no prior experience of motherhood to call on, this must have been difficult for both of them. Sadly, later in life he would be accused of rape, assault and murder, but Kateryn did not forget John, making his wife, Lucy, one of her ladies-in-waiting when she became queen.

Perhaps at this point, Kateryn expected to be able to settle down and get used to her role as wife and stepmother and, for two years, that was indeed the case. But, in 1536, the Latimer's lives were disrupted by religious upheaval, by what is known as the Pilgrimage of Grace. In a sense this was about people rebelling against change and a desire to return to what they knew. To understand the Pilgrimage of Grace, we need to leave Kateryn at Snape Castle and view the religious situation in England, and the upheaval caused by Henry's desire for a male heir.

Notes

1 Porter, Linda, *Katherine the Queen*, p. 60.
2 Ibid., p. 66.

4 The Pilgrimage of Grace

In his desire for an heir, Henry had ended England's subjugation to the Pope so that he could divorce his wife, Catherine of Aragon, and marry Anne Boleyn. He had also supported, for a time, the translation of the Bible into English. People were now told that they could have a direct and personal relationship with God, rather than needing a priest to intercede for them. And this is, indeed, what the Bible teaches us: that Jesus is our great High Priest who offered his life as a sacrifice for our sins and nothing more is needed for our salvation. But in the 1500s, this was a very radical and strange idea. Having been brought up with the Latin mass, confessing sins to a priest and doing penance for sin, men and women were now being told that some of these were no longer necessary. It undermined everything they believed in and this was frightening. Religion was integral to their way of life, but now it was seemingly under threat. All they knew and understood was disappearing in front of their eyes. In June 1536, the King published 'The Ten Articles' which attacked superstition, holy days, pilgrimages and idolatry. Also, monasteries continued to be closed—this process having been started by Thomas Cromwell several years earlier. Monasteries would have been central to the community, and so their disappearance was another aspect of well-known life that was suddenly done away with. A number of Henry's northern subjects arose in protest. The aim of the pilgrimage was not to overthrow the King, but rather to rid the King of those whom the pilgrims perceived as 'evil counsellors' who influenced him.[1]

So, what exactly happened? In October 1536, having heard that commissioners were about to arrive at their parish church and remove what they saw as signs of God's glory, the citizens of Louth rose up to protect their church and the objects inside, and this spread to other towns in Lincolnshire. These people came from the working classes; led by a shoemaker, there were blacksmiths, weavers and other labourers. They turned into a mob, and disorder spread. On the 5th of October, the mob intercepted a man called Robert Aske, the son of a Yorkshire landowner. Given the choice of either swearing an oath to their cause or dying, Aske took the oath. He then took on a very active role in the rebels' cause and started to co-ordinate communications between the mob and other bands in South Lincolnshire. It is possible that, being a third son with no great prospects and with a lawyer's training, he thought he could both give the rebels a voice, and take on a leadership role which would have been denied him in the normal run of things. This revolt in Lincolnshire subsided in a fortnight, particularly after Henry had threatened them with a huge military force who would 'burn, spoil and destroy their goods, wives and children with all extremity'.[2] However, Robert Aske continued with his mission and raised up other areas of the country, such as Yorkshire. On the 16th of October, he entered York with 10,000 followers. He composed an oath entitled, 'Oath of the Honourable Men', which all men who followed him were to swear. They were to enter the *Pilgrimage* for 'the preservation of the King's person, his issue and the purifying of the nobility and to expulse all villein blood and evil councillors'.[3] They were to 'take before you the cross of Christ and your heart's faith to the restitution of the church and to the suppression of heretics' opinions'.[4] Aske began to co-ordinate a more wide-spread rebellion, and Lord Latimer, Kateryn's husband, had already been caught up in it.

By the 11th of October, the unrest caused by the Pilgrimage was coming close to Snape, where Latimer and Kateryn lived, and soon Latimer took the pilgrims' oath. What Kateryn may have thought of this is uncertain as, while her husband was conservative in matters of religion, the Parr family were committed to the monarchy and her brother, William, was showing an interest in religious reform. So she may have had conflicting loyalties. Soon, Latimer and Lord Lumley were leading an army of between 30,000 and 50,000 men towards London. Their aim was to march on London, remove those who were seen as evil counsellors around the King, and convince Henry to turn back the clock and change the religious direction of England. But they failed. God's Reformation was not to be turned back so easily. Thomas Howard, the Duke of Norfolk, confronted the rebels at Doncaster and assured the rebels that their demands would be heard in London, that they would be pardoned, and that there would be a sitting in Parliament to discuss their grievances. Two of the rebels' leaders, Sir Robert Bowes and Sir Ralph Ellerker, would go back with Norfolk to the King to present the petition, and it was agreed that the rebels would do no more until their two leaders returned. (In persuading the rebels to disband, it may be that Norfolk saved Henry's throne, as a battle against the rebels would not have been one that Norfolk could have won.) Deciding to play for time, the King and his advisors issued a general pardon to the rebels, and Bowes and Ellerker returned with only verbal assurances. At this time, Latimer was very visible as a spokesman and negotiator for the rebels and Aske, but he was not really trusted by either side. Henry VIII and Cromwell viewed him as unreliable, and the rebels could not be entirely sure about those they had coerced to take the oath.

The delay, caused by the pardons, created divisions among the leaders and they met in York to decide what to do. They sent various resolutions to Norfolk. However, on the 27th of November, the King himself replied to the resolutions with a letter full of threats, particularly against Aske, with whom he was furious. Again, the rebels met in Pontefract to set out their resolutions more fully. The Archbishop of York, who up to this point had been able to avoid siding with either the King or rebels, was asked to preach, particularly on whether it was lawful for men to take up arms against their sovereign prince. They sought religious justification for what they were doing, but instead the Archbishop said that it was not lawful for men to bear arms without their sovereign's permission and he had to be removed for his own safety. However, the men drew up the Pontefract articles which outlined very clearly what the rebels wanted. They wanted the 'heresies' of Luther, Wycliffe and Hus and other reformers destroyed, and the authority, which was currently Henry's as head of the church, to be returned to Rome. Another meeting was held between Norfolk and the leaders, including Aske and Latimer. Realizing that a military solution was not an option, they were again promised a Parliament and a pardon. Satisfied with this, and believing that Henry would keep his word, the rebels dispersed.

Latimer was now in a difficult position, having taken sides with those who rose up against the King. His most important aim was to get back in royal favour. However, by trying to please both rebels and King, he pleased neither. Henry ordered Latimer back north to prepare for military duties on the Scottish border, and the unrest rumbled on beneath the surface. Some were concerned that Latimer's attempts to curry royal favour were actually signs of betrayal, and so, in January 1537, when Latimer was away from home, a mob stormed Snape Castle, and took Kateryn and her two stepchildren, Margaret and John, hostage to act as surety for Latimer's continued allegiance to their cause. In a letter written on the 20th of January, Latimer wrote that 'the commons of Richmondshire, grieved at my coming up [to London] have entered my house at Snape and will destroy it if I come not home shortly. If I do not please them, I know not what they will do with my body and goods, my wife and children.'[5] This must have been a very frightening and worrying time for Kateryn, as her husband had gone to clear his name and yet, by doing so, was putting her and the children in more danger. (It is unlikely that Kateryn would have been assaulted by the mob, as those involved in the Pilgrimage had very clear rules of conduct.) However, Latimer did return and the mob soon dispersed.

Sadly, the Pilgrimage ended in many deaths. Sir Francis Bigod, a knight from East Riding, who wanted Henry to give up his royal supremacy over the church, was perhaps more perceptive than others involved. He did not trust Henry's words and so took up arms to try and enforce the Pontefract articles. Norfolk was sent to the North again and, this time, declared martial law, proceeding with multiple executions. This included Aske, who had actually taken no part in this latter part of the uprising. Also, the monasteries, which the rebels had tried to protect, were all dissolved, as they were now seen as hotbeds of dissent. Their intention had been to make Henry better and to get rid of those who were apparently being a bad influence, although in the end they only succeeded in making him worse, with many killed for their part in the uprising.

But what about Latimer who had, like Aske, been a leader in the *Pilgrimage*? He was imprisoned in the Tower of London, but fortunately he was perhaps not seen as important enough to be executed. Also, he had various influential friends and relatives, such as William Parr, his brother-in-law, who had served well under Norfolk. However, Latimer had now lost his reputation and would always need to be vigilant not to upset the King. To keep in Cromwell's good books, he had to pay Cromwell sums of money, which forced him to sell some of his property. (This may have been another reason for his survival; after all you do not kill off the golden goose!)

Kateryn's part in the Pilgrimage of Grace had been a very uncertain one and, when taken hostage, a very frightening one. But there was one happy outcome for Kateryn. She and Latimer moved south to Wyke in Worcestershire and then on to Stowe Manor in Northamptonshire to distance themselves from the troubles they had been mixed up in. It also meant that Latimer could be nearer to the court, as he would now need to be careful to stay on the right side of Henry and Cromwell. Kateryn was nearer to the family she had always been close to. She was also perhaps more comfortable in the familiar South, rather than in the 'rough' North lands.

Chapter 4

Notes

1 Porter, Linda, *Katherine the Queen*, p. 86.
2 Ibid., p. 85.
3 Ibid., p. 86.
4 Ibid., p. 86.
5 Ibid., p., 104.

5 Kateryn's choice

Now in the South and nearer to the court, Kateryn became a regular visitor there. Her brother, William, had been made a baron in 1539, and her sister, Anne, who had been lady-in-waiting to both Jane Seymour and Anne of Cleves (Henry's third and fourth wives) was a prominent lady of the court. This would have been a good point of introduction for Kateryn, and she would soon become a lady-in-waiting to Princess Mary, Henry's daughter.

Then, in 1543, Lord Latimer died, aged fifty, having had declining health since September of 1542. On the 2nd of March, he was buried in St Paul's Cathedral. In his will, he gave Kateryn his manor at Stowe and estates near York. She was also given the responsibility of bringing up his daughter, Margaret, and should Margaret not marry within five years, Kateryn would be given further support to look after her. Tragically, as we have already noted, Margaret was to die young.

Kateryn was now a widow for the second time. However, this time she was financially comfortable and might even be able to make her own choice of husband—no longer forced by circumstances to choose a rich husband to ensure her survival, as she may have been at the time of her second marriage. While she was living at court, there was one man who particularly caught Kateryn's eye: Sir Thomas Seymour. So, who was this potential husband?

Sir Thomas Seymour was the brother of Jane Seymour, Henry's third wife, who had finally provided Henry with his longed-for heir, Edward. The marriage of their sister, Jane, brought both Thomas and his brother, Edward, to prominence at court. Thomas himself was appointed to the Privy Chamber and knighted in October 1537, around the time of his nephew's christening. Sadly, Jane died very shortly after Edward's birth. Due to the two brothers continuing at court after this and being uncles to the future king, the family stayed in favour after Jane's death. Thomas was given minor employment in the court, continuing on good terms with the King. He was a very desirable catch—a ladies' man who played up to his charms and his reputation of being the most dashing blade at court. He enjoyed being at sea and was credited even by his enemies as being personally brave. He was ambitious, but not a pious evangelical. Although it is not certain when Kateryn first met Thomas, it is possible she met him through her brother, William, who had known both Thomas and his brother, Edward, from childhood.

However, another suitor came into the picture, and he was not really a suitor one would say no to—Henry VIII. To understand Henry, once again, we need to leave Kateryn and look at his life up to this point.

Henry's backstory

Henry VIII was the second son of Henry VII, who had won the crown from Richard III at the Battle of Bosworth. This was part of the Wars of the Roses which had seen the families of York and Lancaster fight over who should rule. Henry VII, a Lancastrian, married Elizabeth of York to cement his position and had eight children with her, four of whom lived to adulthood—Arthur, Henry, Margaret and Mary. Margaret was married to James IV of Scotland and became the grandmother of Mary, Queen of Scots. Mary was married firstly to

Louis XII of France, and then to Charles Brandon, the Duke of Suffolk. Mary's daughter, Frances, was the mother of Lady Jane Grey, the nine-day Queen of England, whom we will meet later in the story. Arthur, Prince of Wales and heir to the throne, was married to Catherine of Aragon, but died after just three months of marriage. Henry VIII had later gone on to marry Catherine himself, after coming to the throne in 1509 aged seventeen. After six births, Mary was the only surviving child of their marriage. The other five had either been stillborn or died in early infancy—including two boys. The previous attempt to put a woman on the throne of England, back in 1135, had been a disaster, prompting near civil war. So, Henry wished to secure his family's claim on the throne with a son, preferably two (in case the first one died, as had happened with his brother Arthur). Also, he wished to marry Anne Boleyn, one of Catherine of Aragon's ladies-in-waiting and an evangelical Christian. This resulted in what is referred to as, 'The King's Great Matter'. The Church of England was formed, and the Pope was no longer acknowledged to have the authority he once did—now being referred to in England as the Bishop of Rome. Despite this, Henry still remained a Catholic, albeit an English one. Although he got rid of some of the Catholic Church's beliefs, such as pilgrimages, he still retained the mass and the doctrine of transubstantiation— where the bread and wine are said to change into the actual body and blood of Christ. Anne Boleyn was no more successful than Catherine of Aragon in producing the much-needed male heir; her only surviving child was Elizabeth. Anne was falsely accused of treason and incest and was executed at Tower Green. It is not possible here to go into all the ins and outs of those fraught years, but Colin Hamer's book, *Anne Boleyn*[1], published by DayOne, is extremely helpful in giving Anne her rightful place in history.

Henry then married Jane Seymour, who, as has been mentioned, produced the longed-for heir, Edward. Sadly, she died in childbirth less than two weeks later—something that was common in those days with somewhere between 10% to 30% of women dying in childbirth. Henry's fourth wife was Anne of Cleves—a political marriage to give Henry an alliance with the Lutheran Princes of Germany against the might of Catholic countries. However, the marriage was not a success. Henry did not take to Anne, with the apocryphal story of him calling her a 'Flanders Mare', summing up his opinion very well. (His actual comment at the time was, 'I like her not'.[2]) After six months their marriage was annulled, so it was as if the marriage had never taken place. Also, the need for an alliance was no longer a priority, as France and Spain were now fighting against each other and so would not be turning their attention to England. (Anne remained at the English court, becoming known as 'the King's sister'.)

Henry's fifth wife was Catherine Howard, a cousin to Anne Boleyn, and was described by Henry as his 'rose without thorns'. However, she was found guilty of adultery and, unlike her cousin, these charges were almost certainly true. She was executed and Henry was now looking for his sixth wife—not an attractive prospect for any woman! Well might Christina of Denmark say, when approached to be Henry's wife, that if she had two heads 'one should be at his Grace's service!'[3] (It is possible that this is actually another of history's myths, as is the 'Flanders Mare' saying, but it helps to understand what women may have felt when being considered as a potential bride for Henry.)

Marriage to Henry VIII

So now, Henry's attention turned to Kateryn. She had all the qualities that Henry wanted. Foxe, author of *Foxe's Book of Martyrs*, described her as 'endued with rare gifts of nature, as singular beauty, favour and a comely personage'.[4] She was also well educated—a quality Henry had enjoyed in his second wife, Anne Boleyn. However, although God would use Kateryn to forward his purposes for his people, it is unlikely that Kateryn was an ardent Protestant at this time, as Henry would be unlikely to take, as he saw it, a heretical wife. She was beginning to be in touch with those of evangelical persuasion, but this was only in a small way and not thought worthy of note at the time. After all, being in contact with people was not the same as believing the same theology. Therefore, it is unlikely that any reformers would have put pressure on Kateryn to marry Henry in order to promote the evangelicals at court.

Henry had actually started to make advances to Kateryn before Lord Latimer had finally died—his first recorded gift being on 16th of February, whereas Latimer did not die until the 2nd of March. Kateryn knew all too well that the position of Henry's wife was one fraught with danger and when he proposed she made him wait for an answer. But the thought of refusing probably never occurred to her. Henry was not really the man to say no to! Although the normal mourning period would be a year, it was on the 12th of July, only four months after Latimer's death, that Henry and Kateryn were married in the 'Queen's Closet' at Hampton Court. This is where Henry had married Jane Seymour and Anne of Cleves. It was a small ceremony with around twenty attendees, the licence being issued by Cranmer and the ceremony being performed by Stephen

Gardiner. (It is perhaps one of God's little ironies that Gardiner took the ceremony when, later in the story, he would play a part in a plan to try and arrest Kateryn, due to the evangelical influence she was having over the King! Kateryn's brother was not present, as he was involved in safeguarding the Scottish border, but Anne, her sister, was there with her husband William Herbert. Mary and Elizabeth, Henry's children were also there but were listed in the notarial instrument describing the marriage as 'our King's near relations'.[5] This is because they had been declared illegitimate when Henry separated from their mothers. Their legitimacy would only be re-established the following year. However, their presence could perhaps be seen as an omen of peace, a sign of the family feeling that Kateryn would go on to help create. When asked if he would have the Lady Kateryn for his wife Henry 'with a joyful countenance answered.... "Yea."'[6] Kateryn also said that she was willing to take Henry as her husband. She wrote to her brother eight days after her marriage to tell him what had happened: 'As it has pleased almighty God of His goodness to incline the King's majesty in such wise towards me ... to take me of all others ... to his wife.'[7] This marriage of his sister also helped to promote the career of William. He was made a Knight of the Garter shortly before their marriage and became the Earl of Essex soon after.

So now, Kateryn was queen of England. When Wriothesley, the Lord Chancellor, wrote to the Duke of Suffolk about the King's marriage, he observed that Kateryn was, in his judgement, 'for virtue, wisdom and gentleness, most merit for his Highness'.[8] Wriothesley was an ardent Catholic, but he did not see that there was anything concerning about Henry's new wife. She certainly did not appear to be a new Anne Boleyn, aiding the new evangelical faith. He wished that 'the Lord send them long life and much joy together'.[9] However, God had a plan for Kateryn's life that would see Wriothesley and Kateryn on very different sides, with Wriothesley aiming to perhaps even curtail the life he had previously wished would be a long one. But this was all in the future. At this point, Kateryn was just starting her new life as queen consort and began to create her court.

Writing about Kateryn's life as queen can be challenging as two of the key features of her life—her attitude to her stepchildren and her forming of a reformed circle—are things that developed over the three and a half years of her reign. So, the next few sections will deal with her life thematically rather than chronologically.

Notes

1 Hamer, Colin, *Anne Boleyn: One short life that changed the English-speaking world*, (Leominster: Day One Publications, 2007).

2 Fraser, Antonia, *The Six Wives of Henry VIII*, (Frome: Weidenfeld & Nicolson Limited, 1992), p. 305 – 306.

3 Weir, Alison, *The Six Wives of Henry VIII*, (London: Grove Press, 1991), p. 384.

4 Porter, Linda, *Katherine the Queen*, p. 129.

5 Mueller, Janel, *Katherine Parr: Complete Works and Correspondence*, p. 45.

6 Ibid., p. 43.

7 Ibid., p. 46,

8 Gairdner, J. and Brodie, R. [Ed.], *Letters and Papers Foreign and Domestic of Henry VIII Volume XVIII Part I*, (London, Her Majesty's Stationery Office, 1901), p. 490.

9 Ibid., p. 490.

6 Kateryn and her court

Having become the highest lady in the land, Kateryn gathered men and women around her to create a court as befitted any queen. These people would be her constant companions and give us an insight into the Queen's character by looking at who she elected to be part of her court. Her sister, the Countess of Pembroke, became her chief gentlewoman. The circle that Kateryn created around her contained many who were or would become reformed Protestants themselves, such as Katherine Willoughby, Duchess of Suffolk, and Anne Stanhope, Countess of Hereford. As we will see later, it is very possible when Kateryn became queen that she was not a Christian, but God used his servant, Cranmer, to bring her to a saving knowledge of himself. He then used Kateryn and her court to lead the women there to have a serious preoccupation with religion and sympathize with views that would lead them to be called 'Calvinists' in Edward's reign. But Kateryn did not just gather people around her; she would start to lead her ladies in daily studies in the Bible and a chaplain would come and preach—David Starkey has described it as Kateryn running a Tudor Open University in religion![1] Princess Elizabeth commented on this love of learning in one of her letters to Kateryn: 'knowing the affectuous [earnest] will and fervent zeal the which your highness hath towards all godly learning'.[2] However, this learning did not just result in more knowledge. For one of the ladies, another Katherine, the Duchess of Suffolk, being a part of Kateryn's court was the turning point for her conversion from Catholicism to reformed Protestantism. She would go on to support Hugh Latimer, a Protestant who would become chaplain to Edward VI and martyr during Mary's reign. Latimer's sermons survive because of the Duchess of Suffolk, as they were printed with her backing and support. Indeed, according to Latimer's servant, the Duchess was a comfort to the martyrs and one of God's instruments for the spread of his Word. She had been in attendance on Kateryn and would have joined in the daily studies of the Bible, encouraging Kateryn as Kateryn encouraged her. Indeed, it was through Katherine Suffolk that Kateryn was introduced to Latimer. Francis Goldsmith described Kateryn's court as one where 'every day [was] like Sunday,' and, although not every member of her court was evangelical, the court came to be seen to stand for exceptional piety.[3] Nicholas Udall, a man Kateryn collaborated with on her book projects, noted, 'How carefully ye [Kateryn] seek the kingdom of God in the midst of a thousand occasions which otherwise might withdraw your high estate therefrom.'[4] Kateryn exhorted others to study God's Word. In a letter to Cambridge University in 1546, Kateryn wrote, 'I gently exhort you to study and apply those doctrines as means and apt degrees to the attaining and setting forth the better, Christ's reverent and most sacred doctrine.'[5]

But it was not simply religion that Kateryn focused on. She enjoyed dancing and had many fabulous outfits, both those commissioned by herself and those that had belonged to Catherine Howard. (This is not as macabre as we might think. Rich gowns were valuable pieces of property, and as such not to be quickly discarded.) She had a passion for shoes—one year she ordered a grand total of forty-seven pairs! Her other interests included music, painting, greyhounds and parrots. Kateryn built up a collection of books, valued both for their contents and their beauty. In an inventory of her possessions taken after her death, there is one book detailed as being 'a book of gold, enameled black, garnished with eight-and-twenty small table rubies, and one rock ruby upon the clasp, and on each side of the book, a table diamond'. There is also a book of prayers and a book of Psalms both covered with velvet and 'garnished with gold'.[6]

However, it was not just ladies of the court and Cambridge University who were helped by Kateryn; God used Kateryn as part of his plan for the lives of two young children. Their names? Prince Edward and Princess Elizabeth. As queen, Kateryn had taken the motto, 'to be useful in all I do'.[7] She was to prove the truth of this when looking after Henry's children.

Notes

1 Starkey, David, *Elizabeth: Apprenticeship*, (London: Chatto & Windus, 2000), p. 43.
2 Mueller, Janel, *Katherine Parr: Complete Works and Correspondence*, p. 84.
3 Fraser, Antonia, *The Six Wives of Henry VIII*, p. 377; Porter, Linda, *Katherine the Queen*, p. 166.
4 Mueller, Janel, *Katherine Parr: Complete Works and Correspondence*, p. 93.
5 Ibid., p. 115.
6 Ibid., p. 630.
7 Porter, Linda, *Katherine the Queen*, introductory pages.

7 Kateryn's influence on future monarchs

As well as being the queen of England, Kateryn was also a new stepmother once again—this time to three children who would grow up to be rulers in their own right. However, this was a very dysfunctional family! Edward was the only child who enjoyed Henry's approval, being the long sought after heir. Mary's relationship with Henry was uneasy and could be upset. Mary was now twenty-seven and had seen her mother go from Henry's beloved wife and Queen to being 'demoted' to Dowager Princess of Wales through an extremely protracted divorce. This divorce had also caused England to move away from the Roman Catholic church of whom Mary was a lifelong adherent. She had been declared illegitimate and made a lady-in-waiting to her half-sister, Elizabeth. Elizabeth was now ten years old but had been only three when her mother had been sent by her father to the block. Edward, six, had never known his mother as she had died only a few days after he was born. They all had separate courts and lived very separate lives from each other. Their previous two stepmothers had not been married to Henry long enough to develop meaningful and helpful relationships before the end of their marriages: Anne of Cleves was only married to Henry for six months, and Catherine Howard had only lasted fifteen months before she was beheaded. Also, at the age of nineteen at the time of her marriage, it is very unlikely Catherine

Howard would have had the skill to be the loving stepmother that Edward and Elizabeth particularly needed in their tender years.

But Kateryn was different. Having already taken on the role of stepmother to Margaret Neville, Lord Latimer's daughter, this meant she now had experience she could draw on to help her with Edward and Elizabeth. God had been preparing Kateryn for the vital role she would now perform. Edward, as the future king, would influence the shape and destiny of the country, so those who influenced him would also have an impact on the future of England. Kateryn's influence now started to reveal itself as, during the Christmas of 1543, the family was recorded as all being together in the same household for the first time. The children would go on to show the love that they had for Kateryn in the letters they wrote to her. Elizabeth wrote of the 'daughterly love' she had for Kateryn and Edward referred to Kateryn as his 'dearest mother', addressing her as though she was actually his birth mother.[1] Kateryn was someone that the children could look up to and would listen to, as she helped to foster good relations in this family. The fact that Mary and Elizabeth had attended the marriage of their father to Kateryn was a good sign that things may now improve. Considering the history between Henry and his two daughters, it was certainly a major accomplishment to get all the family together. Henry now started to refer to his offspring as his 'dearest children' and, in 1544, when he went to France, in one of his letters to Kateryn, he asked her 'to give, in our name, our hearty blessings to *all* our children' [italics mine].[2] Therefore, in a loving family with a caring mother and a better relationship with their father the children could flourish. On the 14th of January 1544, Mary and Elizabeth were both declared legitimate; no longer Henry's 'near relations', as they had been called in the record of his marriage, they were now Henry's daughters once again. Chapuys, the Spanish ambassador, wrote to Charles V, Mary's cousin, that 'the Queen favours the Princess [Mary] all she can and ... has constantly urged the Princess' cause.'[3] It has been suggested that, because Kateryn saw her possibility of having a child with Henry was slim (Henry's weight and other health problems meant it was very unlikely), she decided to focus on Henry's existing children.[4]

Although not always able to see the children face to face, she wrote to them and sometimes used her stepdaughter, Margaret Latimer, as a go-between. Unfortunately, only one letter from Kateryn to the children survives: one to Edward. However, as we have the letters the children wrote to her, it is possible to work back and gain some understanding of what Kateryn may have said in her letters and her general attitude to the children.

Edward (later Edward VI)

Edward was six at the time of Henry's marriage to Kateryn. What might have been his feelings as his father got married yet again? There had not been much time to build up a relationship with his previous two stepmothers, but Kateryn was different. In Edward's letters, he frequently refers to Kateryn as 'dearest mother' and in one letter he thanks her for treating him kindly when he was at Westminster: 'Such benign treatment suffuses the coldness in me so that I love you more.'[5] He wanted to please Kateryn, explaining in one letter that his reason for not writing to her for a long time was not due to negligence but rather 'that I should write more accurately

... as you want me to progress in all goodness and piety'.[6] Kateryn was encouraging Edward in his studies and so, he desired to do well to please her. In his letters there was nothing to suggest that Kateryn was not his birth mother—a testimony to how much love and care Kateryn showed to him.

But Edward was not just a little boy in need of a mother's love. He was to be the next king of England. She was clearly aware that her impact on Edward would not just affect him, but a whole nation. Edward wrote a thank you letter to Kateryn in January 1547, for a gift of a double portrait of Henry VIII and Kateryn. When Kateryn replied to his letter, she hoped that the gift would spur Edward on, so that he would 'distinguish both [himself] and this commonwealth'.[7]

However, it was not just through her letters of encouragement that Kateryn had an impact on the future king. Edward and Elizabeth had various tutors and each one was committed to the Reformation and to the Biblical doctrine of salvation. These men included Richard Cox, John Cheke, Roger Ascham, William Grindal and Anthony Cooke. Richard Cox had been chaplain to both the King and Cranmer, and would go on to become Dean of Westminster Abbey. He helped to draw up the prayer books of 1549 and 1552, both of which were Protestant in their theology—the 1552 prayer book clearly rejecting the ideas of the mass and transubstantiation. John Cheke was the greatest Greek scholar of the age and made Cambridge University the centre for reformed religion. He would remain close to Kateryn for the rest of her life and would later be knighted by Edward, in 1552. Cheke also called on the help of Roger Ascham, who would later become Elizabeth's tutor after the death of the previous tutor, William Grindal, from the plague. Anthony

Cooke was probably not an official tutor but more of a companion. He was granted an annuity of £100 for providing training in good letters and manners to Edward. These men, teaching Edward and Elizabeth day in and day out, would be able to direct their minds to godly things and instruct them in the teachings of the Bible.

But did Kateryn have any say in the appointment of these tutors? Henry was certainly not a man to be easily influenced and the subject of his son's tuition was an extremely important one. Also, Henry was surely not the kind of man to publicly record, whether in letter or in speech, that he had taken anyone's advice, especially from a woman. So, we do not have the categorical evidence that Kateryn chose or helped to choose these godly men. In consequence, historians have widely differed in their opinions, ranging from Kateryn actively choosing these men to her not having either the ability or the learning to be able to do so.[8] However, when Kateryn was proclaimed regent, Henry gave detailed instructions as to who was to be in Edward's court, including appointing Richard Cox and John Cheke 'for the better instruction of the prince'.[9] It could be that the timing of this, when Kateryn would be there to oversee these instructions, indicates that she had some advisory impact. Kateryn certainly took an interest in Edward's education and so probably knew and approved of the appointments. These tutors would go on to help Edward and Elizabeth advocate the principles of reformed religion. God used these tutors to form a man and a woman who would lead his people forward in following him, when they became monarch of England.

Edward began to think for himself and his letters show a godly man starting to emerge. In one letter to Kateryn, he wrote, 'The only true consolation is from heaven, and the only real love is the love of God.'—this from a boy who was only nine years old at the time![10] He was also concerned that others should be kept from the evil one. In the same letter he wrote, 'Preserve ... my dear sister Mary, from all the wiles and enchantments of the evil one; and beseech her to attend no longer to foreign dances and merriments which do not become a most Christian princess.'[11] Although we may not agree with dances being from the evil one, we can at least appreciate that God had changed Edward through his tutors and Kateryn's influence. He was now one whose whole life was dedicated to God, who knew the truths of the Bible, and who wanted to save others from what he saw as the temptations of the evil one. Edward's letters show that Kateryn encouraged him to continue in his studies. Edward wrote, 'that it [the letter] may be a testimony of love to [her] and of [his] study'.[12] Edward was anxious to show his stepmother that he was diligently learning. This interest is most apparent in one of Edward's earlier letters from 1545, when he writes that Kateryn's letters to him give 'much comfort and encouragement to go forward in such things wherein your grace beareth me on hand that I am already entered'.[13] Kateryn had been praising Edward for qualities he does not yet possess, hoping that it would spur him on to gain that quality, a tactic often used by Renaissance counsellors of the day. If, as some historians have said, Kateryn was not educated enough to choose tutors, this phrase from his letter shows that she was at the very least helping Edward to work hard in his learning by providing incentives.[14] In the same letter, Edward wrote that he prayed he would be able to 'satisfy the good expectation of the King's majesty ... and your grace [Kateryn]'.[15] These expectations from both Henry and Kateryn provided Edward with the motivation to do well in his studies—studies that would lead to him becoming the first truly reformed king of England. Did we not find, as children, that encouragement from our parents and our teachers would spur us on to do better? Kateryn took a very personal interest in Edward's education, inspiring him in his Protestant studies, providing him with some valuable reasons to do as best he could.

The reformed Protestantism that would result from Kateryn's encouragement and Edward's tutors would be one that would lead John Foxe to compare Edward with King Josiah of the Bible.[16] Josiah was king of Judah after a time of great spiritual depravity. He repaired the temple and got rid of the idols, set up by previous kings. The Book of the Law, most likely the book of Deuteronomy, was rediscovered and read out to the people and they celebrated the Passover after a lapse of many years. (The story of his reign can be found in 2 Kings 22–23 and 2 Chronicles 34–35.) Edward, in his turn, would allow the Bible to be read in English by all people and he got rid of much of the decoration found in churches. Some historians tend to look at Edward's getting rid of images as destruction, as many works of art were lost—now there are only a few examples of pre-Reformation art. But we need to remember that those images were possible distractions from the preaching of God's Word. People might worship them instead of the God who gave them the ability to make them. So, Edward wished to get rid of them, not because of their artistic value, but because God's Word was more important than anything else.

The two reigns of Edward and Josiah were considered so similar that Foxe wrote, 'No odds are to be found, but only in length of time and reign' (Josiah reigned for thirty-one years whereas Edward only reigned for five).[17] In Edward's reign, reformed Protestantism moved forward, something that can be partly attributed to Kateryn's influence on him. So, although indirect, Kateryn's influence on the Reformation through Edward was considerable.

Elizabeth (later Elizabeth I)

Kateryn was one of the most influential women in Elizabeth's life, particularly from the ages of nine to fifteen. She had godly tutors, as did Edward, and would have been encouraged by Kateryn in her letters. Additionally, Kateryn was a supportive stepmother and mentor to Elizabeth. It was unlikely that Elizabeth would remember her own mother, as she was only two and a half when Anne Boleyn was executed. Her three previous stepmothers had been more concerned with forging bonds with Mary. But, again, it was different with Kateryn. For example, in one letter Elizabeth wrote that she knew 'your highness's clemency has had as much care and solicitude for my health as the King's majesty would have had'.[18] This was written when Elizabeth and Kateryn had spent at least a year apart, and yet Kateryn still had concern for Elizabeth, caring for her despite the distance that separated them. Kateryn had also ensured that she mentioned Elizabeth to Henry every time she wrote to him (this was during a period when Henry was in France). Again, as with Edward, Elizabeth refers to herself as Kateryn's daughter who 'revere[s] [Kateryn] with daughterly love'.[19] There is no obvious mention of the fact that Kateryn is not her mother. Kateryn's previous relationship with the daughter of her second husband stood her in good stead for this time. So, we can see God had been preparing Kateryn for this role as she had experience of being a stepmother. Margaret testified in her will of Kateryn providing her with a 'godly education and tender love' and it is probable that Elizabeth would have been able to testify to something similar.[20] But, Elizabeth was no ordinary stepdaughter. Margaret would die at the age of twenty-one, and be largely forgotten by history, but Elizabeth would go on to become one of the most famous queens of England, overseeing a so-called 'golden age'.

Through Kateryn, Elizabeth gained an appreciation of scholarship and culture, but she also gained far more than this. God used Kateryn to bring Elizabeth into contact with Protestant beliefs, give her an understanding of them and perhaps even contributing to her conversion. One particular way we can see this is through a book published at the time called *Mirror of the Sinful Soul*. This book was written by Margaret of Navarre, sister to Francis I of France, who was mightily used by God to help Protestants in Roman Catholic France.[21] A French edition of this book appeared in 1531, and Elizabeth decided to translate the book into English for Kateryn as a 1544 New Year's Day gift, knowing that the volume was a favourite of Kateryn's and would bring her pleasure. But what was the message of the book? Elizabeth gives a very simple *précis* in a letter she wrote to Kateryn, which accompanied the book: Margaret 'doth perceive how of herself and of her own strength she can do nothing that good is or prevaileth for her salvation, unless it be through the grace of God ... trusting also that through His incomprehensible love, grace and mercy, she ... doth faithfully hope to be saved'.[22] This truly is the message of the Bible—we can do nothing for our salvation through our works, but must fully rely on Jesus' atoning

Chapter 7

work on the cross for forgiveness of our sins. As Kateryn's stepdaughter, Elizabeth was being exposed to reformed teaching, and was able, despite her tender age of ten, to summarize the great theme of justification by faith in just two sentences. Elizabeth now understood the principal idea of reformed doctrine: justification by faith alone.

Despite not saying what she thought personally of the doctrine in her letter, Elizabeth, in her own reign, would refer to Catholicism as a 'false and erroneous doctrine'. She went on to create a period in English history where Protestantism was allowed to flourish. A prayerbook, produced in 1559 in Elizabeth's reign, was very similar to the one produced in 1552, which was reformed in its doctrine. Elizabeth proclaimed herself the Supreme Governor of the Church of England, undoing Mary's attempt to bring the country back under the authority of the Pope. When a bishop made the mistake of raising the bread of the Lord's Supper in her presence, Elizabeth's response was to immediately storm out! At the end of Elizabeth's reign, the only theology one could access was that of Protestantism. As with Kateryn, we cannot be certain of someone's salvation from this distance. God is the only one who knows the state of Elizabeth's soul, but we can certainly see that the teachings she received in childhood had a major impact on her. Perhaps this translation project was to show Kateryn clearly that Elizabeth now believed the things Margaret of Navarre had set out in her book?

Mary (later Mary I)

Mary was a different matter from Elizabeth and Edward. Partly this was due to her age. She was twenty-seven when Henry married Kateryn, and so, Mary's character and beliefs were already formed.

As with the other two children, Kateryn cared for Mary, demonstrating her concern in letters such as one in 1545 where she wrote, 'nothing quite so much moves me as care for your health'.[23] She expressed a hope that Mary would be able to visit, saying that 'nothing will be a greater joy or a greater pleasure'.[24] They shared similar interests, such as scholarship and dancing. However, this relationship was of a different sort from that with Edward and Elizabeth. Mary was an adult and only four years separated her and Kateryn. So, rather than a mother-child relationship, it was more that of sisterly affection. Later on, we shall be looking into one of Kateryn's book projects—that of translating *Erasmus' Paraphrases upon the New Testament* into English. Mary was persuaded by Kateryn to translate the Gospel of John. When Kateryn wrote to Mary to discuss whether she would allow her name to be put on the book, she wrote that she would 'leave this whole matter to [Mary's] prudence'.[25] Kateryn was not trying to direct Mary as much as the other children. Moreover, although she referred to Edward as her son in her letter to him, Mary is not called 'daughter', but rather 'lady', indicating the relationship is not one of parent and child, but rather one of friendship.[26]

So, what did this mean for Kateryn's influence on Mary? Kateryn thought that Mary's religious beliefs might be alterable and that some gentle pressure would turn Mary away from her Catholic beliefs to more reformed ones. Edward also believed that Kateryn would be able to have this influence over Mary. As we have seen, in 1546 he wrote to Kateryn asking her to preserve Mary 'from all the wiles and enchantments of the evil one' and to stop her from attending dances.[27] However, despite Kateryn's efforts, including exposing her to God's Word with the translation project, Mary never renounced her Catholic beliefs. When she came to the throne in 1553, she attempted to bring the English church back under the authority of the Pope and burnt around 300 Protestants as heretics. Why did God not use Kateryn to bring Mary to saving faith? With our limited knowledge and minds we cannot tell. However, it is true that the comparison of Mary's shorter, bloodier reign with Elizabeth's 'Golden Age' rule would lead to England, as a country, tending more towards Protestant doctrines. What we can be assured of is that God's purposes are always right and true and are the best for us. Though some might see Kateryn as a failure in not persuading Mary to turn to the Protestant faith, or at least to a less ardent pursuit of her Catholic beliefs, this was God's plan for both of them and for England.

Notes

1 Mueller, Janel, *Katherine Parr: Complete Works and Correspondence*, p. 82 and p. 125.

2 Kujawa-Holbrook, Sheryl, 'Katherine Parr and reformed religion', *Anglican and Episcopal History*, Vol 72, No 1, (Appleton, Wisconsin: Historical Society of the Episcopal Church, 2003), p. 69; and Mueller, Janel, *Katherine Parr: Complete Works and Correspondence*, p. 70.

3 James, Susan, *Kateryn Parr: The Making of a Queen*, p. 131.

4 Borman, Tracy, *Elizabeth's Women: The Hidden Story of the Virgin Queen*, (London: Jonathan Cape, 2009), p. 87.

5 Mueller, Janel, *Katherine Parr: Complete Works and Correspondence*, pp. 117, 119.

6 Ibid., pp. 125–126.

7 Ibid., p. 127.

8 Scarisbrick, J. J., *Henry VIII*, (London: Yale University Press, 1997), p. 457; Dowling, Maria, 'The Gospel and the Court: Reform under Henry VIII' cited in: Lake, Peter and Dowling, Maria (Eds), *Protestantism and the National Church in the Sixteenth Century*, (New York: Routledge, Kegan & Paul, 1987), p. 61.

9 Mueller, Janel, *Katherine Parr: Complete Works and Correspondence*, p. 50.

10 Ibid., p. 116.

11 Ibid., p. 116.

12 Ibid., p. 121.

13 Ibid., p. 86.

14 Dowling, Maria, 'The Gospel and the Court: Reform under Henry VIII', p. 61.

15 Mueller, Janel, *Katherine Parr: Complete Works and Correspondence*, p. 86.

16 Foxe, John, *The Acts and Monuments of John Foxe*, Cattley, Stephen [Ed.] (London: R. B. Seeley and W. Burnside, 1837), p. 698–699.

17 Foxe, John, *The Acts and Monuments of John Foxe*, p. 699; 2 Chronicles 34, *The Holy Bible: New International Version* (London, International Bible Society, 1984), p. 476.

18 Mueller, Janel, *Katherine Parr: Complete Works and Correspondence*, p. 82.

19 Ibid., p. 82.

20 Porter, Linda, *Katherine the Queen*, p. 60.

21 For more information about Margaret, please read: VanDoodewaard, Rebecca, *Reformation Women: Sixteenth-Century Figures Who Shaped Christianity's Rebirth*, (Grand Rapids: Thomas Nelson, 1982), p. 29–39.

22 Mueller, Janel, *Katherine Parr: Complete Works and Correspondence*, p. 85.

23 Ibid., pp. 86–87.

24 Ibid., pp. 87–88.

25 Ibid., p. 88.

26 Ibid., p. 126, p. 86.

27 Ibid., p. 116.

8 Regent of England

Having taken on the role of stepmother, Kateryn was now called upon to take on a much more important role, that of regent of England. Near the beginning of his reign in 1513, Henry had gone to fight in France, leaving his wife, Catherine of Aragon, as regent. Now, thirty years later, he was departing once again for France, having declared war on France in the summer of 1543 in an alliance with Charles V, the Holy Roman Emperor, who was a Spaniard. Henry strongly disliked Francis, the King of France, and he also wished to defend English rights in France—a concern that had been shared with many of his predecessors, particularly Henry V, who had famously defeated the French at Agincourt in 1415.

So, it was now another Catherine, Kateryn Parr, who would take on the mantle of regent while her husband went to France. She was appointed regent on the 11th of July 1544 and 'ruled' till the middle of September—a period of two and a half months. But Henry did not leave her without advisors. On the 7th of July, Henry and his Privy Council took a series of resolutions setting out how the country was to be governed during Henry's absence. Half of the Privy Council were to stay with Kateryn, and half were to go with Henry. Cranmer, the Archbishop of Canterbury, Wriothesley the Lord Chancellor, Edward Seymour (Jane Seymour's brother), Stephen Gardiner and Sir William Petre were all named as men whom Kateryn would 'use the advice and counsel of', but the most significant of these men has to be Cranmer.[1] He would attend her daily during this time—something that God used as part of his plan to bring Kateryn to himself. She had perhaps received Protestant teaching in the household of her first father-in-law, as he had a Protestant chaplain. However, as we shall see later from the book *Psalms or Prayers*—a translation project she was involved in—she still most probably held some Catholic beliefs at the time of the project, and it would be unlikely for Henry to marry an 'heretical' wife. But God did not leave Kateryn in her sins. She was now in frequent contact with Cranmer, a man who was developing more and more in his own evangelical beliefs and would indeed become one of the martyrs of Mary I's reign. After this time, we see Kateryn becoming more and more reformed in her writings, so it is possible this was the time she was converted. Humanly speaking, had there been no regency or if Cranmer had not been one of her advisors, Kateryn may not have been saved. But God was in control and worked out his plan to save her.

This period of regency helps us to understand a vital point of her marriage with Henry—what did they feel for each other? We may be tempted to see Kateryn as marrying Henry against her will and spending three and a half years pining for her true love, Thomas Seymour. But this is not the case. Although it may have been a different type of love to the feelings that she had for Thomas, the letters from this time show that Kateryn and Henry certainly had affection for each other. Writing to Henry in France, Kateryn would say, 'The want of your presence, so much beloved and desired of me, maketh me that I cannot quietly pleasure in anything, until I hear from your majesty.'[2] To assure Henry that these were her true sentiments and not just words written on paper, she wrote that 'God, the knower of secrets, can judge these words not to be only written with ink, but most truly impressed in the heart'.[3] Although many today sadly take God's precious name in vain, in those days to invoke God's name was a very serious thing and would have assured Henry that Kateryn was in earnest when she wrote her loving letter. Henry, too, used terms of affection when referring to his wife. When decreeing that Kateryn would be regent, he referred to her as 'our most dearest and most entirely beloved wife', as well as calling her 'sweetheart' in one of his letters in 1544.[4] Indeed, the very fact that Kateryn was the one chosen as regent, showed the trust and respect Henry had for her and for her judgement. He would not have gone off to fight in France without leaving the country in safe hands and this was what he considered Kateryn to be. England was to be ruled by a woman! (Apart from Catherine of Aragon, the only other woman to try and rule in her own right was Matilda back in 1135 and, as already mentioned, this had led to something on the scale of a civil war.)

This was no easy task for Kateryn to be given. The country was now at war; there were plague and religious divisions to be dealt with; and the constant problem of the Scottish border with the threat of conflict from that country. When Henry went to France in 1513, the Scots had used the opportunity to invade. Fortunately for England, at that time the victory had gone to them and had resulted in the death of James IV, but there was no surety that the same would happen this time. Edward VI had been betrothed to Mary Queen of Scots through the Treaty of Greenwich and yet, Henry had started a torch and burn campaign against the Scots along the border. This was still in progress when Kateryn became regent. However, Kateryn not only survived but established herself; a tribute to the capability that God had given her. Kateryn followed her husband's orders and requests and kept the home fires burning. She oversaw the supplies needed for the war and commanded that various aids be sent to Henry—ordering £40000 and then £20000 be sent to Henry in France as well as gunpowder and shot. Kateryn kept Henry well informed about the situation at home, telling him on one occasion that some Frenchmen and Scots had been captured in Rye; she sent highly confidential letters, that had been found on them, to Henry so that he 'might thereby certainly understand the crafty dealing and juggling of that nation'.[5] (As France and Scotland were allies, it would be important for Henry in France to know what Scotland were up to.) Then, she also made various orders concerning affairs at home. In July, she declared that all Frenchmen had to prove they were allowed to be in England and, if not, they were to avoid England.[6] She ordered that a debt owing to her be paid, and in September ordered that no one who had the plague should come to court 'upon pain of her grace's indignation, and further punishment at her highness' pleasure'.[7] In Scotland, under the command of Edward Seymour, the army attacked both Edinburgh and Holyrood Palace. The Earl of Lennox, a Scottish noble, defected to the English side, and Kateryn wrote to tell Henry, wishing Lennox all success now that he was serving 'such a master whom God doth aid' [Henry].[8]

Of all the influences that Kateryn had on Elizabeth, the most important was encouraging her in reformed doctrine, as it concerned her eternal soul. But there was another impact Kateryn had on Elizabeth that was crucial when her time came to ascend the throne. Elizabeth saw that it was possible for a woman to rule in her own right.

Today, it is not unusual for us to have a woman on the throne. Both Queen Victoria and Queen Elizabeth II became the longest reigning monarchs in their lifetime. So, we perhaps fail to understand why the idea of a woman ruler would cause such consternation. But, in Tudor times, as historian Helen Castor puts it, 'man was the ruler of woman, and the king was ruler of all. How, then, could royal power lie in female hands?'[9] But now, both Mary and Elizabeth saw a woman rule in a time of adversity and do it well. Mary was related to women who had done this, as her mother, Catherine of Aragon, had been regent and her grandmother, Isabella of Castile, had reigned jointly with her husband Ferdinand of Aragon in Spain. But Elizabeth had only seen her father rule and would have been raised to see women as the weaker sex. Now she was able to observe Kateryn ruling with confidence over a country at war with France and threatened by conflict with Scotland, and saw that she did this while managing to avoid a catastrophe.

This period would leave a strong impression on Elizabeth, as she saw that a woman could handle the job as well as a man. Elizabeth's own rule would be that of the 'virgin queen', as she did not marry and ruled in her own right, needing no man at her side. The adult Elizabeth was a product of the influence of Kateryn and it has been suggested that Elizabeth's reign and strong leadership were Kateryn's longest lasting achievement.[10] Indeed, Kateryn was highly honoured in Elizabeth's reign, being depicted as one of the virtuous queens of England alongside Esther from the Bible and Elizabeth herself, while Anne Boleyn—Elizabeth's own mother— was not. Elizabeth's Protestant reign came to be seen as a 'golden age', in contrast to Mary's perceived failure, reigning as a Catholic.

This contrast would form England into more of a naturally *Protestant* country. In 1689, the *Catholic* James II was overthrown in favour of the *Protestant* William III and his wife, Mary II, who was James' daughter, because of the worry as to what a Catholic monarch might mean for the country. We have the Church of England today and have a rich Protestant heritage—something that other countries, such as France, do not have. Again, God was working his plans and purposes out through his servant Kateryn. She may have had some idea that Elizabeth would be affected by her, but could she have imagined such a great and long-lasting impact? We can never fully know and understand how God may use us for his purpose, or the impact we may have on others around us, but we should still press on and do his work.

In October, Henry returned home. He had managed to take the town of Boulogne, which surrendered on the 14th of September. However, Henry's ally, Charles V (the king of Spain), was willing to make peace with France by treaty, if at all possible, rather than war, and sued for peace with the French. So, Henry decided to return to England. He was hailed as a war hero, although the money it would take to upkeep Boulogne and Calais—England's other French possession—was very high. (England ended up losing both towns by 1558.) Now her husband had returned, Kateryn could return to her role of queen consort.

Notes

1 Mueller, Janel, *Katherine Parr: Complete Works and Correspondence*, p. 49.
2 Ibid., p. 63.
3 Ibid., p. 63.
4 Ibid., pp. 52–53, p. 70.

5 Ibid., p. 61.

6 Ibid., pp. 54–55.

7 Ibid., pp. 60–61, 70.

8 Ibid., p. 60–61, 66-67.

9 Castor, Helen, *She-Wolves: The Women Who Ruled England Before Elizabeth*, (London: Faber & Faber, 2010), p. 33.

10 Porter, Linda, *Katherine the Queen*, p. 348.

9 *Psalms or Prayers*

D uring her time as queen, Kateryn worked on four literary projects: *Psalms or Prayers, Paraphrases of the New Testament, Prayers or Meditations* and *The Lamentation of a Sinner.* The first one, *Psalms or Prayers,* was a translation of a book produced by John Fisher, the Catholic Bishop of Rochester, and was published in April 1544. This book was not simply a re-production of the Psalms as laid out in the Bible, but rather took various verses from the Psalms; other books of the Bible, such as Isaiah; and occasionally the Apocrypha, to create fifteen 'psalms' on various subjects. For example, one paragraph reads:

'O Lord God, which are rich in mercy, and of Thine especial love towards us, even when we were Thine enemies, by sin, didst send into the world Thine only begotten son Jesus Christ: that whosoever believeth duly in Him, shall not perish, but have everlasting life.'[1]

The last segment will be familiar to many as that of John 3:16, and the first segment draws on Ephesians 2:4–5 and 1 John 4:9. Many other parts of the book are similar, with one sentence drawing on two or three separate verses from various books of the Bible. The fifteen 'psalms' deal with different subjects such as the remission of sins, a prayer for godly wisdom, a plea to be defended from enemies and thanksgiving that the enemies have not 'gotten the overhand of him'.[2] Following the 'psalms' there is a selection of verses from Psalm 22, then Psalm 100, a 'Prayer for the King' and finally a 'Prayer for Men to Say Entering into Battle'. Throughout the book there is a deep humility, knowing that the sinner is not worthy to come before

God. There is a desperate plea for God to save the sinner from his sins and praising God for who he is. The size of the finished book, five inches by seven inches, may indicate that it was meant for personal use, perhaps during household prayers.

However, Kateryn did not simply translate from Fisher's original, but modified it along the way. Fisher's title for his 4th psalm was 'Psalm Four: it is earnestly sought, that one who is oppressed by sins may surmount them.'[3] While the 'psalm' itself does exhort the reader to cry out to God for help, the title gives all the agency to the sinner; this is what *you* do to overcome sin. But Kateryn translated it as, 'The Fourth Psalm is a complaint of a penitent sinner which is sore troubled and overcome with sins.'[4] Kateryn's title is more of a passive one, with the sinner doing nothing but crying out; perhaps because the original one took away from *Christ's* victory over sin. But why make that change? At this time, Kateryn was probably still a traditionalist, believing in the doctrines taught by the Roman Catholic church. On three separate occasions in the book, she used the word, 'penance', meaning oral confession of sin to a priest. When she used this word, she indicated that God only forgives when sinners have performed penance, but there is no mention of this in the Bible. For example, her English translation said, 'Thou hast promised forgiveness of sins ofttimes to them that do penance'.[5] But the change of title for the 4th psalm gives the victory over sin back to Christ. Although not explicitly reformed doctrine, it would seem strange that Kateryn would translate Fisher's titles for all the other psalms as he wrote them but change this one, unless she disagreed with what Fisher had written, or felt it gave an erroneous impression. Perhaps here we can see a slight shift in Kateryn's beliefs. Although still believing in Catholic doctrines, she was starting to have her own thoughts on religion, and God's light was slowly and surely breaking through on her life.

As well as modification, Kateryn also added to the work. 'A Prayer for Men to Say Going into Battle', the last prayer in the book, is her own work. This was Kateryn's first piece of published writing, completed within the first year of her marriage—the timing of which is probably very significant. In only a few months' time after the publication of this work, Henry would set off to make war in France, and so there would be many a man who may wish to utter such a prayer. The prayer reminds God of the victory he gave David over 'the great huge Goliath' and asks God that the enemy might be turned to peace so that 'no Christian blood be split'. Or, if that was not to happen, that there would be little blood split and that 'innocents' (presumably those who lived near the battlefield) would be little hurt or damaged. Finally, the prayer asks that, at the end of the war, all may be joined in unity to the praise of God.[6] This prayer tells us little about Kateryn herself, although it does show her concern for her husband and those that he took with him, who would soon be crossing the English Channel to fight in France.

However, this prayer was significant for another reason. As this was Kateryn's original work, she was now a published author—something it was extremely uncommon for a woman to be at this time—although her name did not appear in the title of the manuscript. Further, this prayer was written in English rather than Latin. Kateryn was showing that she would champion work in the vernacular—something that was becoming more common over time with the Bible having been printed in English by Tyndale and others. This would become even more obvious with a later translation project, that of *Erasmus' Paraphrases of the New Testament.*

Psalms or Prayers was a very successful publication and had gone through eighteen editions by the early seventeenth century—showing that it had a lasting impact beyond Kateryn's death, as people still wished to read or use it long after she had died. This book and her next, entitled *Prayers or Meditations,* helped to fulfil a need for worship books that women, in particular, could use, which would have added to their popularity. Some of the ladies at Kateryn's court received a copy from Kateryn herself. Even Henry approved of the work and, in later printings, it was given the informal title of 'The King's Prayers'. Although Kateryn was starting to slowly shift towards reformed teaching, the book was not so obviously Protestant that it would offend anyone. There was no mention of prayers for the dead or to the saints, but *penance* was still present.

Notes

1 Mueller, Janel, *Katherine Parr: Complete Works and Correspondence*, p.216.
2 Ibid., p. 338.
3 Ibid., p. 264.
4 Ibid., p. 264.
5 Ibid., p. 230.
6 All quotes from Mueller, Janel, *Katherine Parr: Complete Works and Correspondence*, p. 364.

10 *Paraphrases upon the New Testament*

B
oth during the regency period of 1544 and after, Kateryn undertook another literary project: that of overseeing the translation of *Erasmus' Paraphrases upon the New Testament*, which contained the four Gospels and Acts. Kateryn wanted people to understand Scripture and so decided to promote the translation of spiritually valuable works, of which this was one. At this time in England's history, there was not the freedom of access to God's Word as there is today. One of the translators on this project, Thomas Udall, described the people of England as a people 'now a long time sore thirsting and hungering in the sincere and plain knowledge of God's Word'.[1] John Wycliffe had translated the Bible into English in the fourteenth century, but the translation was copied by hand, so large numbers of copies did not exist. He had also used the Latin Vulgate translation, which was not an accurate translation of the Hebrew and Greek. William Tyndale had translated the Bible in the 1520s and 1530s and had been burned at the stake in 1536. Miles Coverdale, who had helped him in his translation, had printed his own version, which borrowed heavily from Tyndale's work. Henry VIII had approved that translation and declared that it should be in every church in the land. However, in 1543, the 'Act for the Advancement of True Religion' was passed, which forbade anyone under the rank of yeoman to read the Bible, including all servants, dependants (children) and women, unless

they came from the nobility or the gentry. By spearheading this translation project, Kateryn showed she wanted more people to be able to read God's Word. Udall spoke of her 'ardent zeal ... towards the promoting of the knowledge of God's holy Word and gospel'.[2] He did have a strong motive to speak well of Kateryn. After all, this was written in a letter to her that prefaced the Gospel of Luke, so he would not wish to criticize her! But, even when that is taken into account, this was a sizeable project, and her later projects and zeal for God's Word would show the truth of Udall's words.

There were four translators: Thomas Udall, one of the earliest Protestant tutors from Oxford, worked on Luke and Acts; Thomas Caius, one of Kateryn's chaplains, who also believed that people should be able to read the Bible and that Christ was the only way to salvation, translated Mark; Kateryn herself translated Matthew; but perhaps the most surprising translator was that of the Gospel of John. It was none other than Henry's daughter, Mary, who was an adamant follower of the religion that had resisted all attempts to translate the Bible into English, persecuting both Wycliffe and Tyndale when they attempted to do so. When Mary fell ill, Kateryn sent her own chaplain, Francis Mallet, to help Mary finish the translation.

This work, when first published, was a very thick book, consisting of one thousand pages. Udall referred to it as 'so sound and substantial meat for all complexions of people'.[3] But, for the work to be published, Henry would have to give his permission, as the Bible was still under restrictive access. Udall was hopeful that Kateryn could use her influence with Henry 'to the same use [Kateryn] hath meant it—that is to say, to the public commodity and benefit of good English people' so that 'he will not suffer it to lie buried in silence'.[4] However, Kateryn does not appear to have had the influence Udall credited her with, and publication was delayed until 1548, in the reign of Henry's son, Edward VI. By this time, people were allowed to read the whole New Testament for themselves, and there were no reprints of the book after 1552—presumably because there was a lack of need for the work. But this is not something Kateryn would have regretted. In his preface to the work, Udall wrote that the book would allow people to 'increase from day to day in knowledge, and also continually be edified in true religion'.[5] Now that people had access to the complete Bible, they could read all of God's Word, and not just select paraphrases. But Kateryn's next publication would not only survive for longer; it would also firmly establish her as a writer.

Notes

1 Mueller, Janel, *Katherine Parr: Complete Works and Correspondence*, p. 97.
2 Ibid., p. 90.
3 Ibid., p. 96.
4 Ibid., p. 97.
5 Ibid., p. 156.

11 *Prayers or Meditations*

Kateryn had now been involved with two literary publications, but *Psalms or Prayers* did not actually carry her name, and *Paraphrases* would not be printed until after Henry's death. However, with *Prayers or Meditations,* published in June 1545, Kateryn was firmly established as the first queen, and perhaps the first woman to ever publish under her own name.[1] When the volume was printed for the third time, it proudly bore the rather long title:

Prayers or Meditations, wherein the mind is stirred, patiently to suffer all afflictions here, to set at naught the vain prosperity of this world, and always to long for the everlasting felicity: Collected out of holy works by the most vertuous and gracious Princess Katherine, Queen of England, France and Ireland.[2]

(For the sake of brevity, it will be called *Prayers or Meditations* from now on!)

The work itself was based on portions of Thomas à Kempis' work, *De Imitatione Christi* (The Imitation of Christ). Thomas à Kempis was a fifteenth-century, German, Christian theologian and his book was considered to be one of the most influential Christian books after the Bible. In it, Thomas encouraged people to reflect on the life of Christ in order to emulate him. However, Kateryn reworked the text to give it a more reformed emphasis. Christ is clearly pictured as the only redeemer—it is 'through Thy grace and by example of Thee', which she later followed up with the statement that 'O Lord, *only* art He that mayest help me' [italics mine].[3] Additionally, she asked the Lord to grant her his grace 'that it may always work in me, and persevere with me unto the end'.[4] It is presented that it is only through the Lord's grace that Kateryn will be able to persevere in Christ till the end of her life. So reformed Protestant teachings are clearly apparent. Yet, there are still some Catholic themes that come across. For example, Kateryn wrote, 'Keep me Lord from sin, and I shall then neither dread death nor hell.'[5] The implication is that it is only when someone stops sinning that they need not fear death. However, Christians believe that, although they continue to sin in this life, they can still trust in Jesus for their salvation and entry into heaven. Therefore, Kateryn would still seem to be relying on her actions in this life to save her in the next to some extent. This perhaps gives us a little of an insight as to Kateryn's spiritual development. As we have seen, *Psalms or Prayers* was more of a Catholic work, as Kateryn used words with particular Catholic connotations like 'penance'. Kateryn's fourth literary project, *The Lamentation of a Sinner,* which we will come to next, was nothing less than a completely reformed statement of faith in Jesus alone. Kateryn was on a spiritual journey from the Catholic beliefs of her childhood to a reformed sinner saved by Jesus' grace alone.

But Kateryn did not just copy, compile and edit *Prayers or Meditations*. Again, she made her own additions in the shape of five prayers at the end of the work, the last four of which may be Kateryn's own work. The first two prayers were the same as the last two prayers in *Psalms or Prayers:* 'A Prayer for the King' and 'A Prayer for Men to Say Entering into Battle'. The third is an expansion of the Lord's Prayer, with Kateryn rephrasing and expanding on what we find in the Bible. For example, instead of 'Lead us not into temptation', Kateryn enlarged on that and wrote, 'Grant O Lord, that we be not utterly led into temptation, that thereby we should be lost. But, in all perils of temptation … let us, Thy children, perceive and feel Thy fatherly succor.'[6] The last two—'Another Prayer' and 'A Devout Prayer'—are both prayers appealing for the Lord's help.

This book was for private worship, compared to works like Cranmer's *Litany*, also published in 1544, which was for more public worship. The books complimented each other very well and, in one printing, Cranmer's *Litany, Psalms and Prayers,* and *Prayers or Meditations* were all published together—something that would not have been done without both the Queen's and Cranmer's consent. This shows that the two books worked well together and had a joint purpose and were possibly further fruit from their close working together, when Kateryn was regent. The work came to be known as 'The Queen's Prayers' just as *Psalms and Prayers* was known as 'The King's Prayers'.

The book was certainly a popular one, going through seventeen to nineteen editions by the end of the sixteenth century (there is some variance between historians).[7] This is possibly due to the fact that the book was so suitable for women—an often-overlooked audience—providing them with manuals of worship they could easily use. As her name was included in the full title of the work, people may also have wished to purchase it so that they may have a book created by a queen. Once again, Kateryn ordered copies of *Prayers or Meditations* to give out to her ladies. This time, however, unlike the very 'safe' theology of *Psalms or Prayers,* the readers would encounter theology closer to what the Bible tells us of how a sinner becomes right with God. The work was re-printed only once during Mary's reign but was printed four times in Edward's reign and nine times during Elizabeth's reign. But it was still palatable to a Catholic, to a certain extent. Elizabeth chose this book as the book she would translate for her father as a New Year's Day present, and it is very unlikely that Elizabeth would have chosen a book with which her father might disagree. We would not give our fathers a gift they might hate, and you certainly would not want to do that with the explosive Henry VIII!

Notes

1 A lady called Margery Kempe had a book created in her own name in the 1450s, but she used scribes to create her work, as well as not being a printed work.
2 Mueller, Janel, *Katherine Parr: Complete Works and Correspondence*, p. 396.
3 Ibid., pp. 399, 409.
4 Ibid., p. 397.
5 Ibid., p. 398.
6 Ibid., pp. 419–420.
7 James, Susan, *Kateryn Parr: The Making of a Queen*, p. 218; Perry, Maria, *The Word of a Prince: A Life of Elizabeth I*, (Woodbridge: Boydell Publishers, 1990), p. 19.

12 The Lamentation of a Sinner

U p to this point, all Kateryn's literary projects had been mostly translations and been taken from other men's writings. But during Henry's reign, Kateryn worked on a completely original piece of writing and, on the 5th of November 1547, after Henry's death, it was published. Its full title was, *The Lamentation of a Sinner, made by the most virtuous lady Queen Katherine bewailing the ignorance of her blind life*.[1] It is a window into Kateryn's very own soul. Although not a biography, in the sense that it does not give us dates and times as to when she was saved, it clearly shows that Kateryn has been changed by God from someone who was blind to someone who can see clearly spiritually and is trusting in God, and God alone for her salvation.

The book begins with a preface by William Cecil, a man who would go on to become Elizabeth I's chief advisor. He explains to the reader that here is the 'wonderful mystery of the mercy of God, a heavenly practice of regeneration'.[2] He encourages the readers to learn from Kateryn's example and know that if we '[ac]knowledge our sins, God is faithful to forgive us, and to cleanse us from all unrighteousness', as the apostle John wrote in 1 John 1:9.[3] Our God has not changed, and we too can know Kateryn's experience and be cleansed from our sins before God.

Kateryn describes her former life in very vivid terms. For example, she wrote, 'when I consider … mine *obstinate, stony* and *untractable* heart' and 'what cause now have I to *lament, mourn, sigh* and *weep* for my life, and time so *evil* spent' (italics added).[4] In the past, she had not considered the blood of Christ sufficient for the cleansing of her sins, and so 'sought for such riffraff as the Bishop of Rome [the Pope] hath planted in his tyranny and kingdom'.[5] (An act called the *Act in Restraint of Appeals*, passed in 1533, meant that the Pope thereafter had to be referred to as nothing more than the Bishop of Rome.) She had thought that she walked in the 'perfect and right way, having more regard to the number of the walkers than to the order of the walking'.[6] This perhaps echoes Jesus' own words in Matthew 7:13: 'broad is the road that leads to destruction and many enter through it'. But, as Kateryn describes it, the mercy of God is 'infinite' and 'unmeasurable', and he did not leave Kateryn in her sinful condition.[7] Now she could write boldly that she had 'no hope nor confidence in *any* creature, neither in heaven nor earth, but in Christ, my whole and only saviour'(Italics added).[8] Furthermore, by writing that 'neither shall this saint or that martyr help us' on the Day of Judgement, Kateryn went against Catholic teaching that saints and martyrs had righteousness that could be imputed to sinners, and went further by saying that all other helpers be 'but vain and counterfeited saviours'.[9] Her hope was to be saved through Christ's blood alone and then to hear God say on the Day of Judgement, 'Come hither, ye blessed of my Father, and receive the kingdom of heaven.'[10] There is no mention of *penance* in this last book, as there was in the first, and there is a plea to those who were not saved, to become so through the blood of Christ *alone*—one that still speaks to its readers today, if we are willing to listen. This book is certainly worth reading! The benefits are great: 'all fear of damnation is gone from them'.[11] Those who followed the teachings of the Catholic church could never be entirely certain whether they had done enough. Had they seen enough relics, said enough masses, done enough penance? And even then, they may still have to experience purgatory—a middle place between heaven and hell where, it was believed, sinners were purged of their sins and made righteous for heaven. But Kateryn then, and Christians today, know they will be declared righteous on the last day, not because of what they have done, but because of what Jesus has done for us on the cross.

While Kateryn had written this book during her marriage to Henry, it was only published ten months after his death, and it is perhaps not hard to see why. Kateryn's book was a clear proclamation of Protestant teachings and did not agree with Henry's English Catholic beliefs. *Lamentation* was published in the reign of her stepson, Edward VI—a boy who would have agreed whole-heartedly with what Kateryn had written. For example, at one point Kateryn writes that it is our duty 'to procure and seek all the ways and means possible to have more knowledge of God's word'.[12] She wanted God's Word to be read by all, as evidenced by her translation project of *Erasmus' Paraphrases*. In Edward's reign, prayer books and preaching were done in English, so all could understand.

This book was unique for its time. Kateryn opened her soul for all to see something that would have hugely astonished her readers, particularly as this lady had been queen of England, the highest lady in the land. Even today, when we have an abundance of Christian biographies and autobiographies, there is a surprising bluntness about the way Kateryn described herself. She would have agreed with the apostle Paul and called herself the worst of sinners, as he does in 1 Timothy 1:15. *The Lamentation of a Sinner* did not circulate as well as *Psalms or Prayers* or *Prayers or Meditations* but it was still a popular book. This may have encouraged others, especially those who were concerned about their own sins, to seek faith in Jesus too.

Through Kateryn's books, we can see how God was teaching her throughout her life. In her first work, *Psalms or Prayers*, penance is mentioned—the idea that we need to do something to earn forgiveness. But now, Kateryn declares boldly before all, that she believes in Christ and Christ alone for her salvation. However, Kateryn's publications and theological leanings were gaining her some unwelcome attention from those in the Catholic camp and, like Esther, she would experience a near brush with death.

Notes

1 Mueller, Janel, *Katherine Parr: Complete Works and Correspondence*, p. 443.
2 Ibid., p. 444.
3 Ibid., p. 445.
4 Ibid., pp. 443–485.
5 Ibid., p. 450.
6 Ibid., p. 449.
7 Ibid., p. 448.
8 Ibid., p. 454.
9 Ibid., p. 465.
10 Ibid., pp. 484–485.
11 Ibid., p. 479.
12 Ibid., p. 476.

13 Near arrest

'**D**ivorced, beheaded, died. Divorced, beheaded, survived.' This will be a familiar little rhyme to many of us, telling us the outcome of Henry's six wives. But the ending could have been very different had God not intervened to save his servant. At one point in her life, Kateryn was nearly arrested for her new God-given beliefs.

As we have seen, Kateryn had built up a court of Christian ladies, had been working on projects that would help ladies with their private devotions, and was also using her influence with her stepchildren to foster Protestant beliefs in them. She even had some influence on Henry. She managed to get him to recall Edward Seymour from his post in Newcastle where he was securing the border with Scotland, after being appealed to do so by Edward's wife. There was also Cambridge University. In November of 1545, certain acts had been passed to further dissolve various specified religious foundations, including colleges, and their assets would then be given to the crown. Those at Cambridge University were concerned about their future and they wrote to Kateryn appealing for help. She replied, 'I according to your desires attempted my lord the King's majesty for the stay of your possessions.'[1] Henry decided to deliver the Cambridge colleges from being dissolved and even went on to found Trinity College in 1546. Kateryn's letter appears to imply her influence was the main reason for this.

But this influence was causing serious concern to some, particularly among those who were Catholics. As we saw earlier,

Wriothesley the Lord Chancellor, had been very complimentary about Kateryn when she was first married to Henry, wishing them a long life together. Now he and others wished to bring Kateryn down. The reason for this was that, having been made regent when Henry went to France, there was a strong possibility that Kateryn may be made regent should Henry die before Edward reached maturity. It would then be very likely that her strong *Protestant* influence would continue. Along with this, it would also be more probable that Edward Seymour, Edward VI's uncle, would also have power, meaning that religious reform would be continued in England—he being evangelically minded as well. The Catholics at court were alarmed by this prospect, but if Kateryn could be degraded somehow, then the influence of the Protestant party at court would suffer a severe setback. Yet, how could they seek to bring down Kateryn, the King's 'sweetheart' and 'beloved wife'?[2] The Catholic party had previously attempted to bring down Archbishop Cranmer, but their plans had failed because Henry had great regard for Cranmer. So, like the administrators and satraps of Daniel 6, they decided the best way to go about this was through Kateryn's beliefs.

At first, they tried through a woman called Anne Askew. Anne had been converted through the reading of the Bible (as a gentlewoman she was permitted to do this, but only by herself, and not with others). She was involved in an unhappy marriage and had moved to London, possibly to try and get a divorce. There she was supported by various ladies of the court, having connections to them through various members of her family. Anne was very outspoken in her biblical beliefs and was arrested, examined and imprisoned in March 1545, the main accusation being her denying the doctrine of transubstantiation –that the bread and wine of the mass was the true body and blood of Jesus. When later examined on the issue of her marriage, she was also examined again by Stephen Gardiner on the sacrament. Having been released, she was again imprisoned in Newgate in 1546 and in April was tried and sentenced to burn. Now, her opponents tried to use Anne to bring down the ladies of Kateryn's court and Kateryn herself. Anne was tortured in such a brutal way that later, when burnt, she could not stand up as all her bones were broken. Anne was pressured to name those women who had maintained her when she moved to London. Association with a known heretic would have been extremely dangerous for these ladies, and would have damaged Kateryn's cause, causing ruin for many, if not all of them. However, Anne refused to name any ladies, only going so far as to say that the men who had brought her aid *reported* to be from Lady Denny and Lady Hertford. But this would not suffice for the Catholic plotters. Anne testified to God's helping hand at this time: 'My Lord God, I thank his everlasting goodness, gave me grace to persevere, and will do, I hope, to the very end.'[3] God did indeed help his servant, and even though under extreme pressure and torture to recant or name ladies, Anne did neither. God protected Kateryn and his people at court.

The plot against Anne Askew had failed to incriminate Kateryn and her ladies, so now Gardiner and Wriothesley tried another plan. A secret search of her room was carried out, looking for heretical books. None were found, presumably because some of her ladies or her uncle, Sir William Parr, had managed to hide them. As an act had been passed on the 8th of July 1546 which proclaimed that any person who hid a Tyndale New Testament or 'such English books as contain pernicious and detestable errors and heresies' would be fined and imprisoned at 'the King's pleasure', such a discovery could have been extremely dangerous for Kateryn.[4] William Parr, her uncle, took the Testament and other books into safe-keeping, and these were only reclaimed three months after Henry's death. Having continued with her studies of the Bible and hearing her chaplain preach every afternoon, Kateryn was emboldened to talk more with Henry about spiritual matters and the reformed faith. Chancing to be present at such a conversation between Kateryn and Henry, and seeing Henry's displeasure, Gardiner 'thought, that if the iron were beaten whilst it was still hot ... such misliking might follow towards the Queen, as might both overthrow her and all her endeavours'.[5] He stoked up Henry's displeasure with Kateryn, and drew parallels between Kateryn's beliefs and sedition; after all those beliefs taught that people should have all things in common, and would try to disavow the government of princes. And so, Gardiner persuaded Henry to draw up a warrant for her arrest. Having been 'browbeaten' by Anne Boleyn, Henry did not wish to be so again and, by publishing works and bringing around her a growing number of supporters, Kateryn was exceeding her authority as Henry's queen.

So, Kateryn needed to be brought down. But Kateryn came to hear about the warrant—how we are not sure. It is possible that Henry told his doctor, who then passed on the news to Kateryn. The other, more exciting version is that the arrest warrant was dropped by accident, found and brought to Kateryn. Either way, God moved so that Kateryn heard about the warrant before it could be executed. Kateryn became hysterical, and 'fell incontinent into a great melancholy and anger'.[6] Had not two of Henry's wives been arrested and beheaded? Now it was entirely possible that the same thing could happen to her. Henry, hearing of Kateryn's distress came to her chambers and 'refreshed and appeased her careful mind'.7 When Kateryn next came to Henry, he purposefully started a conversation about religion, testing her to see how she would react. However, Kateryn declared that as 'a silly, poor woman' she could do nothing but defer to Henry's judgement in this matter as '[her] only anchor, supreme head and governor here in earth'.[8] Henry contradicted her forcefully, saying that she had become a doctor 'to instruct [him] ... and not to be instructed or directed by [him]'.[9] But Kateryn dissembled and said that her reasons for talking of religion were only so that she might take his mind off the pains in his leg (Henry had ulcers which had been growing worse over the years), and to learn more from what he said in their conversations. Kateryn could not admit guilt or express sorrow, as to admit guilt was the very thing that had helped condemn Anne Boleyn and Catherine Howard. Thankfully for Kateryn, Henry accepted what she said and declared that 'perfect friends we are now again, as ever at any time heretofore'.[10]

In a comedic turn of events, Gardiner and/or Wriothesley later turned up with a band of soldiers to arrest Kateryn. They were soon sent packing with a royal flea in their ears! The failure of this arrest would leave advocates of reform firmly in places of power. What Henry's motives were behind this episode we cannot be certain. It is possible that he could have been playing games with both sides—wanting to humiliate his councillors by the failed arrest and bring them down a peg; to assure himself of his wife's humility; and to make certain everyone was aware that Henry VIII was still very much in charge, despite his ulcers. Whatever the motivations behind this event, God had protected his servant, as he did when Esther went before Xerxes without permission—an action that could have caused Esther to be killed (Esther 4 & 5).

Kateryn had survived a brush with death, but Henry soon found himself confronting death, as his health started to fail.

Notes

1 Mueller, Janel, *Katherine Parr: Complete Works and Correspondence*, p. 116.

2 Ibid., pp. 53, 70.

3 Porter, Linda, *Katherine the Queen*, p. 264.

4 Gairdner, James and Brodie, R. H. (Ed.), *Letters and Papers, Foreign and Domestic of the Reign of Henry VIII, Volume XXI, Part I*, No. 611, p. 1233. https://www.british-history.ac.uk/letters-papers-hen8/vol21/no1. [accessed 11 September 2023].

5 Foxe, John, *The Acts and Monuments of John Foxe*, p. 555.

6 Foxe, John, *The Acts and Monuments of John Foxe*, p. 558.

7 Foxe, John, *The Acts and Monuments of John Foxe*, p. 558.

8 Mueller, Janel, *Katherine Parr, Complete Works and Correspondence*, p. 24.

9 Ibid., p. 24.

10 Foxe, John, *The Acts and Monuments of John Foxe*, p. 560.

14 Henry's death

On January 27th, 1547, Henry lay in his bed suffering from his last illness. No one had dared to tell Henry before, that he might be dying, but now Sir Anthony Denny told the King that 'in man's judgement, you are not like to live'.[1] Archbishop Cranmer was sent for, but when he reached the King, Henry could no longer speak. Cranmer asked Henry if he was 'trusting in the Lord', and to give some sign with his hand.[2] According to Foxe, 'the King, holding [Cranmer] with his hand, did wring his hand in his as hard as he could'.[3] In the early hours of the 28th of January 1547, Henry VIII, who had judged and condemned so many, was called to give an account at God's greater judgement seat.

What was Henry's spiritual state at this time? On the 29th of May 1543, a book was published that was nicknamed, *The King's Book*, due to Henry's approval of the work. In this book, the doctrine that man was and is saved by faith *alone* and not by any works he can do, was firmly rejected. Furthermore, Henry began his will by stating, 'trusting that every Christian who dies in steadfast faith and endeavours ... to do such good deeds and charitable works ... is ordained, by Christ's passion, to eternal life'.[4] He believed he could add to his salvation by doing good works, which is not taught in the Bible. Henry's changes to the Church in England had been motivated, not by wanting to reform the church and bring it back to the teachings of the Bible, but by his own needs. The need for a divorce had brought about the break with Rome and the dissolution of the monasteries helped to fill his treasury. None of these things had been motivated by a desire to bring the English Church back to the true tenets of the Bible. Cranmer had only asked Henry if he trusted in the Lord, not whether he was trusting in the Lord *alone*. So, it could be that Henry was trusting in the Lord, but also trusting in the good deeds that he had done, and for the masses he had ordered to be said for his soul in his will. Was Henry saved—a true son of God? The short answer is that we cannot tell, as only God can see into men's souls. We will never know the answer until we enter heaven ourselves, and mark either Henry's absence or his presence.

While doctors, and various men who were vying for power, had gathered around Henry's deathbed, there was one notable absentee—Kateryn. She would only come to Henry when he sent for her, but Henry never did so. She had last seen him just before the Christmas of the previous year but, since then, Henry had only had men around him. There are two possible reasons for this absence. One is that no one had the bravery to tell Henry he was dying until only a few hours before his actual death. In 1534, a treason act had been passed saying that any who did 'maliciously wish, will or desire, by words or writing or by craft imagine' the King's death were guilty of treason.[5] If Henry were to recover, he might not be favourably disposed to the person who had said he was dying, and they could have been convicted under this act. So, Henry was possibly not aware, until a short time before, that he was dying and so had no chance to send for Kateryn. But there was perhaps another more political reason at work. Edward was only nine, and so there would need to be a regency until he was eighteen, when it would be supposed that he would be capable of ruling in his own right. In 1544, Kateryn had been made regent and it was possible that she might be so again. Had Kateryn been at Henry's side, she could have moved Henry more towards her ideas and to order the regency in her favour. This would have meant that none of the men, such as Edward Seymour, would have the significant power they longed for. So, it was imperative to keep Kateryn out of the way in Henry's final days. The man who eventually emerged with most of the power was Edward Seymour, brother-in-law to Henry and uncle to the now King Edward VI. Henry had decreed in his will that there would be a collective form of government but, instead, Edward Seymour became 'Lord Protector' – apparently with agreement from the Privy Council. Kateryn now found herself the 'Dowager Queen of England' with riches, lands and properties but with no presence in the corridors of power, or any political agency. We can only imagine what Kateryn thought of this—perhaps disappointed, upset and angry at being cast aside? She had lost a husband whom she cared for deeply and had been ousted from a role she may have thought was hers after the regency of 1544.

And so, Kateryn found herself a widow for the third time in her life. On the 16th of February 1547, Kateryn watched Henry's funeral service from the Queen's closet in St George's Chapel, Windsor Castle. (He was buried alongside his third wife, Jane Seymour.) But her position now was far removed from when her first husband had died. Then she had been friendless with little or no income. Now Henry's will made her a very wealthy woman. She was granted £10000 worth of plate, jewels and household goods, as much apparel as she wanted to take away and still had her possessions of Hanworth and Chelsea. Henry had declared that all this was a reward for Kateryn's 'great love, obedience, chastity of life and wisdom'.[6] Henry had clearly valued the last of his wives. No longer was there any need to marry for money or a comfortable way of life, as these were already hers. She was at last able to make her own choice and, for Kateryn, there was only ever one man for her.

Notes

1 Porter, Linda, *Katherine the Queen*, p. 271.

2 Foxe, John, *The Acts and Monuments of John Foxe*, p.689.

3 Ibid., p.689.

4 Gairdner, James and Brodie, R. H. (Ed.), *Letters and Papers Foreign and Domestic of the Reign of Henry VIII Volume XXI Part II*, No. 634, p. 320. https://www.british-history.ac.uk/letters-papers-hen8/vol21/no2

5 Smith, Lacey and Morrill, John, 'The Break with Rome', *Britannica*, online edition. https://www.britannica.com/place/United-Kingdom/The-break-with-Rome#ref482974

6 Fraser, Antonia, *The Six Wives of Henry XIII*, p. 396.

15 Marriage to Thomas Seymour

Now having the freedom to make her own choice for perhaps the first time in her life, having had enough of duty, she decided to pursue a relationship with Thomas Seymour, King Edward's uncle, who had had to give way to King Henry four years earlier. In a letter to Thomas, written about a month after Henry's death, Kateryn declared that 'My mind was fully bent [in 1543] to marry you before any man I knew.' But God 'made me to renounce utterly mine own will, and to follow his will most willingly' by leading her into marriage with Henry.[1] She had obeyed, but now Henry was dead. And so, they began courting. However, it was all done in secret. Thomas was very careful with whom he discussed his relationship with Kateryn. In one of his letters to Kateryn, he told her how he had even been circumspect when talking with her sister, Anne, until he realized that Kateryn had already told her about their relationship.[2] Anne Parr and her husband, William Herbert, went on to become go-betweens between the two lovers. Kateryn once wrote to Thomas that 'I dare not desire to see you for fear of suspicion' and also commanded him that he should throw her letters into the fire—although she soon took back this instruction.[3] The admirable Queen who had been so careful and considerate in what she did when married to Henry, now became a woman whose sole focus was to marry the man she loved, regardless of the consequences.

They were married only months after Henry's death. We do not know the exact date; it probably took place around the end of May.

But herein lay a problem. Firstly, the speed at which they had got married defied the conventions of the day. Although Henry had married Kateryn only four months after Latimer's death, that was different. After all, Henry was the King. But as Dowager Queen, Kateryn should have been in mourning for at least a year and not rushing into marriage again. This is perhaps why they kept the courtship secret. More importantly, although extremely unlikely, it was theoretically possible that Kateryn could have been carrying Henry's child for nine months after his death. So, through this potential offspring, Kateryn had a claim to the throne as, according to Henry's will, any such child would succeed Edward and any heirs he had. In Henry's reign, it had been made treason for someone with a claim to the throne to marry without the Privy Council's permission. No action was brought against Kateryn and Thomas at this time, but the hasty marriage brought about other unfortunate consequences: Kateryn's relationships with Edward and Mary began to sour.

As we have seen, Edward had a deep regard for his stepmother and would write to her often, showing her affection and a concern for what she thought of him. God had used this relationship to consolidate the Protestant beliefs Edward held. However, things had now changed. Edward was king, and so had many different duties to occupy his time. As a result, there were fewer letters from Edward to Kateryn. In July 1548, John Fowler, one of the members of the Privy Chamber, wrote to Thomas Seymour saying that 'If his grace [Edward] could get some spare time, [he] would write a letter to [Kateryn] and to [you].'[4] After Kateryn's marriage, there are only two letters—the first simply detailing her love for him and his for her. The last is just a note from Edward, included in the letter from John Fowler. The note simply read, 'My lord, I thank you, and pray you to have me recommended to the Queen.'[5] This is quite a difference from the long letters Edward had previously written to Kateryn. Although it is possible that the shift was due to his increased responsibilities and that he may have considered it wrong to address someone as 'mother' when he was her king; yet, it is also an indication that Kateryn's influence had gone from that of a loving mother, actively involved in his education, to simply a lady married to his uncle. Now Kateryn had no contact with her nephew/stepson.

Kateryn and Thomas wanted Edward to approve of their marriage, and so decided to try and trick the King into thinking that he had been the architect of their relationship. Thomas bribed Fowler, a member of the Privy Council, to speak to Edward for him and to put into his head the idea that Thomas should marry Kateryn. Fowler set about this by asking Edward who he thought Thomas should marry. However, things did not go the way they expected, as Edward first suggested Anne of Cleves (Henry's fourth wife), and then, his sister Mary. In fact, Fowler had to go so far as to suggest Kateryn to him. Fortunately for Thomas and Kateryn, Edward was led to believe that he had brought about the match, writing to thank Kateryn on the occasion of her marriage for 'your gentle acceptation of our suit'.[6] However, this relationship had been going on before Edward had taken any interest in it and, when Edward found out what had actually happened, he was reportedly displeased. The woman who had meant so much to him was now scheming and even going so far as to use him for her own ends. Had this attempted dupe been successful, Kateryn and Thomas may have been able to control the young King, but it actually had the opposite effect, as there was a shift in the tone of Edward's letters to Kateryn after this. As noted above, the letters were fewer and he no longer referred to her as 'mother'.

Kateryn's relationship with Mary also underwent a change. Mary wrote to Thomas Seymour referring to the marriage as 'strange news', and she refused to play any part in helping the marriage along.[7] The friendship between the two ladies was now at an end, meaning any influence came to an end as well.

Elizabeth was the least affected by this marriage as she actually went to live with Thomas and Kateryn; and there was a further addition to their household—Lady Jane Grey. Jane was the great niece of Henry VIII, being the granddaughter of his youngest sister Mary. As the daughter of the Marquis of Dorset (later Duke of Suffolk), she would be considered valuable as a marriage prospect. Thomas secured her wardship from her parents for £2000 (around £1.7 million today[8]) and so, she came to live with Kateryn—the idea being that Thomas could obtain a good marriage for Jane, perhaps even that of marriage to King Edward himself. It may seem strange to our modern way of thinking to seemingly sell your daughter, but such provisions for those of the aristocracy was common in those days. Had Thomas succeeded in this marriage plan, he would have hoped to gain more influence for himself at court, for Kateryn and Thomas had been trying to gain more power in court circles but had had little success. The suggested marriage never happened, but God had his purpose for Jane in this new household. Kateryn was able to nurture the Protestant faith that Jane already had and, when debating various doctrines of faith with high figures of the Catholic faith in 1554, Jane, with the Holy Spirit's aid, was able to hold her own, despite being only fifteen.

Kateryn's marriage to Henry had been a happy one with good relationships with her stepchildren. Unfortunately, this was not the case with Kateryn and her new brother- and sister-in-law, Edward and Anne Seymour. Between the two women particularly there was no love lost. For example, there was the problem of precedence. Who was first lady of the land—the wife of the Lord Protector who effectively ruled the land, or the former wife of the last King? And Kateryn was not particularly complimentary about Edward Seymour either. Writing to Thomas describing a meeting between her and Edward, she said, 'It was fortunate we were so much distant, for I suppose I should have bitten him!'[9] Sadly, Edward did nothing to help the relationship, as he was holding back Kateryn's jewels, given to her by both Henry and her mother, Maud. Kateryn had sent them to the Tower of London for safekeeping when she went into mourning for Henry. However, Edward would now not give them to her. Her struggle for power had not been successful, and these arguments over precedence and jewels allow us to see that Kateryn was by no means perfect, as a temper not so evident before, now comes to the fore.

Notes

1 Mueller, Janel, *Katherine Parr: Complete Works and Correspondence*, p. 131.

2 Ibid., p. 137.

3 Ibid., pp. 140, 133.

4 Ibid., p. 172.

5 Ibid., p. 174.

6 Ibid., p. 147.

7 Ibid., p. 146.

8 This is according to the Inflation calculator on the Bank of England website, correct at the time of this publication: https://www. bankofengland.co.uk/monetary-policy/inflation/inflation-calculator.

9 Mueller, Janel, *Katherine Parr: Complete Works and Correspondence*, p. 141.

16 Family matters

As Elizabeth continued to live with Kateryn, the assertive queen that she would go on to become became more obvious. In January 1548, her tutor, William Grindal, died of the plague. Kateryn wished to appoint Francis Goldsmith, one of her own supporters. But Elizabeth wanted a different man—Roger Ascham, of whom Grindal had been a protege. Elizabeth was successful in carrying her point and Roger Ascham was duly appointed. But did this mean that Kateryn's influence with Elizabeth was waning? It would seem so, but that is not quite true. Ascham was a Protestant and continued to teach Elizabeth regarding religious matters—the same beliefs as she had been taught up to this point. The fact that Elizabeth would want a man of Protestant persuasion is a testimony to Kateryn's early influence as stepmother. Having had that key influence in Elizabeth's early years, it was now paying off. Unfortunately, Elizabeth soon left Kateryn's household to try to avoid scandal involving Kateryn's husband, Thomas.

Thomas Seymour was very much a ladies' man and it would appear that Elizabeth developed a crush on him. Had that been the end of it, we might not have known about it 500 years later but, unfortunately for all parties concerned, it was not. Thomas started to engage in horseplay with Elizabeth, but it evolved into something much less innocent. For example, he cut up Elizabeth's dress (while she was wearing it), with Kateryn holding Elizabeth. He would enter her apartments before she was dressed in the morning, and rumours started to circulate at court about their relationship. This was dangerous for Elizabeth, particularly as her mother had been executed on charges of adultery with other men, showing what could happen to a woman who was not circumspect in these matters. So, Kateryn sent Elizabeth away to Lady Denny, the sister of Elizabeth's governess. We need to remember with this episode that there was no such thing as 'adolescence' in Tudor times. At fifteen, she was of marriageable age, and so rumours of these incidents with Thomas Seymour would put her in danger and harm any prospects of a good marriage.

It is hard to know what to make of this episode. Our main source for this is depositions made at a later date when Thomas Seymour was arrested for treason, in January 1549. They were made by Katherine Ashley, Elizabeth's governess, who was not the most reliable source. She was known to be indiscreet and fond of gossip and both she and Kateryn were potential rivals for Elizabeth's affections. So, we cannot be sure how much of her testimony is completely true and how much may have been embellished. Kateryn's taking part in Thomas' play is very strange. It is possible that, as she was now pregnant, her hormones were clouding her judgement, or the love she had for her husband blinded her to what she was complicit in. In truth, no one comes out of this story well. But it does serve to remind us that Kateryn was not a perfect saint and was tainted by her sinful nature, as we all are.

Peace was soon made between Kateryn and Elizabeth, and Elizabeth noted in one of her letters that '[Kateryn] would warn [her] of all evils that [Kateryn] should hear of [Elizabeth].'[1] But they never saw each other again, for God was to call his servant home just three months later.

Notes

1 Mueller, Janel, *Katherine Parr: Complete Works and Correspondence*, p. 171.

17 Kateryn's death

Kateryn was now six months pregnant and she and Lady Jane Grey moved to Sudeley Castle in Gloucestershire. On the 30th of August 1548, Kateryn gave birth to a girl, who would be named Mary. However, while the baby was healthy, Kateryn soon became unwell with puerperal fever. This was the fear of every pregnant Tudor woman—a deadly bacterial condition that caused many Tudor women to perish. It was due to the lack of understanding about cleanliness and sterilization that we have now. Sometime between 2am and 3am on the morning of the 5th of September, God called his servant home, and Kateryn died. Having experienced four marriages to four very different men, being taken hostage in the Pilgrimage of Grace, acting as regent of England and publishing four books, Kateryn was now at rest in heaven. However, she did not have any merit before God because of her accomplishments, but because she believed in Christ alone for salvation. She now knows the truth of her own words: 'He [Christ] has delivered us from the condemnation of sin, from the bondage of the law, from the fear of death, from the danger of the world, and from all the evils in this life, and in the other to come.'[1]

Having been the first queen to be published, she now became the first member of the royal family to be buried with Protestant funeral rites. It was especially stressed at the funeral that the offering taken was only done to help the poor and would not benefit Kateryn's soul in any way. Likewise, the candles lit and placed around her corpse were solely for the honour of her and for no other reason, such as shortening her time in purgatory. The service was led by Miles Coverdale, her chaplain, who had aided William Tyndale in translating the Bible into English. To all in attendance or those who read the anonymous narrative that has come down to us, it was very clear that this funeral was different to all those that had gone before. Psalms and a *Te Deum* were sung in English, not Latin. Her tomb can now be seen in the church at Sudeley Castle, with the following inscription: 'Here Lyethe quene Kateryn, Wife to Kyng Henry the VIII and Last the wife of Thomas Lord of Sudeley, high Admyrall of Englond and onkle [uncle] to Kyng Edward the VI, dyed 7 September M. CCCCC.WLVIII [1548].'[8] [The date given is actually the date of her funeral.]

Her daughter, Lady Mary Seymour, would soon disappear from historical record. She was sent to live with Kateryn's good friend, Katherine, the Dowager Duchess of Suffolk. However, after the age of two, nothing more is heard of her. Infant mortality rates were very high in Tudor times, so it is very likely that she died as a toddler.

Notes

1 Mueller, Janel, *Katherine Parr: Complete Works and Correspondence*, p. 465.
2 Ibid., p. 182.

18 What happened next?

What happened to the other main players in Kateryn's life after her death? In her will, she gave all she had to her husband, Thomas Seymour, but he was not content to simply be a rich man and still hungered after more power and control over the King. He tried to ingratiate himself with Edward by giving him more pocket money (Edward had little to spend on his own amusements) but failed to get Edward to sign a bill making him 'Governor of the King's person'. Thomas then tried a far more audacious plot to kidnap the young King during the night. Unfortunately, it went badly wrong when the King's dog raised the alarm and Thomas shot the dog dead. He was arrested, tried for treason and executed on the 20th of March 1549. It is fortunate that Kateryn never lived to see her husband fall to such depths.

Edward Seymour continued to introduce more reforms, such as the 1549 and 1552 prayer books with the help of Thomas Cranmer—books that clearly showed the country being steered away from Catholicism to a more reformed understanding of the Bible, rejecting the doctrine of transubstantiation. He was later ousted from power and, when he tried to gather support, was imprisoned and executed in 1552.

When King Edward was dying in 1553, he and the man then in power, John Dudley, Duke of Northumberland did not want Mary to succeed to the throne as, being a Catholic, she would no doubt attempt to undo all Edward's Protestant reforms. In Edward's will they appointed Lady Jane Grey as Edward's successor who, as we have seen, was a reformed Protestant, like Edward. (It was not possible for Edward to simply bypass Mary for his Protestant stepsister, Elizabeth, as the reason given why Mary could not inherit—her being declared illegitimate by Henry—also applied to Elizabeth.) However, Jane only reigned nine days and was deposed when her army was defeated by the army of Mary. She was executed on Tower Green in 1554, but not until she had given a shining testimony to her faith, debating skilfully with leading Catholic theologians of the time. (For more information on this subject, see *Lady Jane Grey, Nine Day Queen of England* by Faith Cook.)

Mary tried to make England Roman Catholic again but, for various reasons, it was not successful. In 1558, Elizabeth then came to the throne, returning the country to Protestantism, although not the strong Protestantism of her brother. She became known as the 'Virgin Queen' due to her decision not to marry and went on to successfully reign for forty-five years, creating what would come to be known as a 'golden age'.

Anne Parr, Countess of Pembroke and Kateryn's sister, died in 1552 leaving two sons and a daughter. Kateryn's brother, William, was favoured with many appointments from Queen Elizabeth I, and, when he died childless and far from wealthy, he was buried at Elizabeth's expense.

Kateryn had a sizeable influence on the Reformation, helping to ensure it continued after her death. Although her influence was a more 'behind the scenes' one, and perhaps not as obvious as other religious figures, such as William Tyndale or Thomas Cranmer, she still deserves to be studied as an integral part of the English Reformation. And perhaps there is a lesson for us from her life? We are not all called to be missionaries or do extraordinary things for God in our life, but God has a work for each of us to do. As Paul wrote in Ephesians 2:10: 'We are God's workmanship, created in Christ Jesus to do good works, which God prepared in advance for us to do.' Kateryn never got to see the entirety of what she had helped to do, not living to see Edward push more reforms through, or Elizabeth rule as queen, but she had laid the groundwork. So, we may never see the full impact of what we have done, but God can use us in our situations for whatever he has planned, even after our death.

Bibliography

Borman, Tracy, *Elizabeth's Women: The Hidden Story of the Virgin Queen,* (London: Jonathan Cape, 2009).

Castor, Helen, *She-Wolves: The Women Who Ruled England Before Elizabeth,* (London: Faber & Faber, 2010).

Cook, Faith, *Lady Jane Grey: Nine Day Queen of England,* (Welwyn Garden City: Evangelical Press, 2004).

Cook, Faith, *Caught in the Web: A Tale of Tudor Times,* (Welwyn Garden City: Evangelical Press, 2006).

Daniell, David, *William Tyndale: A Biography,* (New Haven and London: Yale University Press, 1994).

Dowling, Maria, 'The Gospel and the Court: Reform under Henry VIII', in: Lake, Peter and Dowling, Maria (Eds), *Protestantism and the National Church in the Sixteenth Century,* (New York: Routledge, Kegan & Paul, 1987).

Foxe, John, *The Acts and Monuments of John Foxe,* edited by Stephen Cattley, (London: R. B. Seeley and W. Burnside, 1837).

Frasier, Antonia, *The Six Wives of Henry VIII,* (Frome: Weidenfeld & Nicolson Ltd, 1992).

Gairdner, J. and Brodie, R. [Ed.], *Letters and Papers Foreign and Domestic of Henry VIII Volume XVIII Part I,* (London: Her Majesty's Stationery Office, 1901).

Gairdner, James and Brodie, R. H. (Ed.), *Letters and Papers Foreign* and Domestic of the Reign of Henry VIII Volume XXI Part I, https:// www.british-history.ac.uk/letters-papers-hen8/vol20/no1

Gairdner, James and Brodie, R. H. (Ed.), *Letters and Papers Foreign and Domestic of the Reign of Henry VIII Volume XXI Part II,* https:// www.british-history.ac.uk/letters-papers-hen8/vol21/no2

Hamer, Colin, *Anne Boleyn: One short life that changed the English-speaking world*, (Leominster: Day One Publications, 2007)

James, Susan, *Kateryn Parr: The Making of a Queen*, (Aldershot: Ashgate Pub. Ltd, 1999).

James, Susan, 'Katherine [Kateryn, Catherine] [née Katherine Parr] (1512-1548)', *Oxford Dictionary of National Biography,* (Oxford University Press, 2004), online edition. https://www.oxforddnb. com/display/10.1093/ref:odnb/9780198614128.001.0001/odnb-9780198614128-e-4893

Kujawa-Holbrook, Sheryl, 'Katherine Parr and reformed religion', *Anglican and Episcopal History*, Vol 72, No. 1, (Appleton, Wisconsin: Historical Society of the Episcopal Church, 2003).

Mueller, Janel, *Katherine Parr: Complete Works and Correspondence,* (London: University of Chicago, 2011).

Perry, Maria, *The Word of a Prince: A Life of Elizabeth I*, (Woodbridge: Boydell Publishers, 1990).

Porter, Linda, *Katherine the Queen*, (London: Macmillan, 2010).

Scarisbrick, J. J., *Henry VIII* (London, Yale University Press, 1997).

Smith, Lacey and Morrill, John, 'The Break with Rome', *Britannica,* online edition. https://www.britannica.com/place/United-Kingdom/The-break-with-Rome#ref482974

Starkey, David, *Elizabeth: Apprenticeship*, (London: Chatto & Windus, 2000).

Strickland, Agnes, *Lives of the Queens of England Volume 5*, (London: Bloomsbury Academic, 1845).

VanDoodewaard, Rebecca, *Reformation Women Sixteenth-Century Figures Who Shaped Christianity's Rebirth*, (Grand Rapids: Thomas Nelson, 1982).

Weir, Alison, *The Six Wives of Henry VIII*, (London: Grove Press, 1991).

Withrow, Brandon, *Katherine Parr: A Guided Tour of the Life and Thought of a Reformation Queen*, (Phillipsburg: P & R Publishing, 2009).